CIVIL WAR in the Ozarks

A typical artillery campground as they appeared throughout battlefields of the Ozarks. (A reenactment photo)

CIVIL WAR in the Ozarks

Phillip W. Steele and Steve Cottrell

PELICAN PUBLISHING COMPANY
GRETNA 1996

First printing, July 1993
Second printing, September 1994
Third printing, April 1996

Library of Congress Cataloging-in-Publication Data

Steele, Phillip W.
Civil War in the Ozarks / Phillip W. Steele, Steve Cottrell.
p. cm.
Includes bibliographical references and index.
ISBN 0-88289-988-0
1. Ozark Mountains Region—History. 2. Kansas—History—Civil War, 1861-1865–Underground movements. 3. Quantrill, William Clarke, 1837-1865. 4. James, Jesse, 1847-1882. 5. Guerrillas—Ozark Mountains Region. 6. United States—History—Civil War, 1861-1865-—Underground movements. I. Cottrell, Steve. II. Title.
F417.09S84 1993
976.7'1—dc20 93-18337
CIP

Civil War in the Ozarks map courtesy Ray Toler, Springdale, Arkansas.

Reenactment photos courtesy Mark Kyger, Joe Fortner, Steve and Rhonda Cottrell.

Civil War photo assistance courtesy Steve Weldon, Carthage Civil War Museum, Carthage, Missouri.

Cover illustration: Battle of Carthage *by Andy Thomas, courtesy Andy Thomas and Carthage Civil War Museum*

Manufactured in the United States of America
Published by Pelican Publishing Company, Inc.
1101 Monroe Street, Gretna, Louisiana 70053

To the memory of our ancestors
and early Ozark families
who fought, died, and endured
the hardships of the great
Civil War and the contribution
they made toward building
the Ozark society we enjoy today.

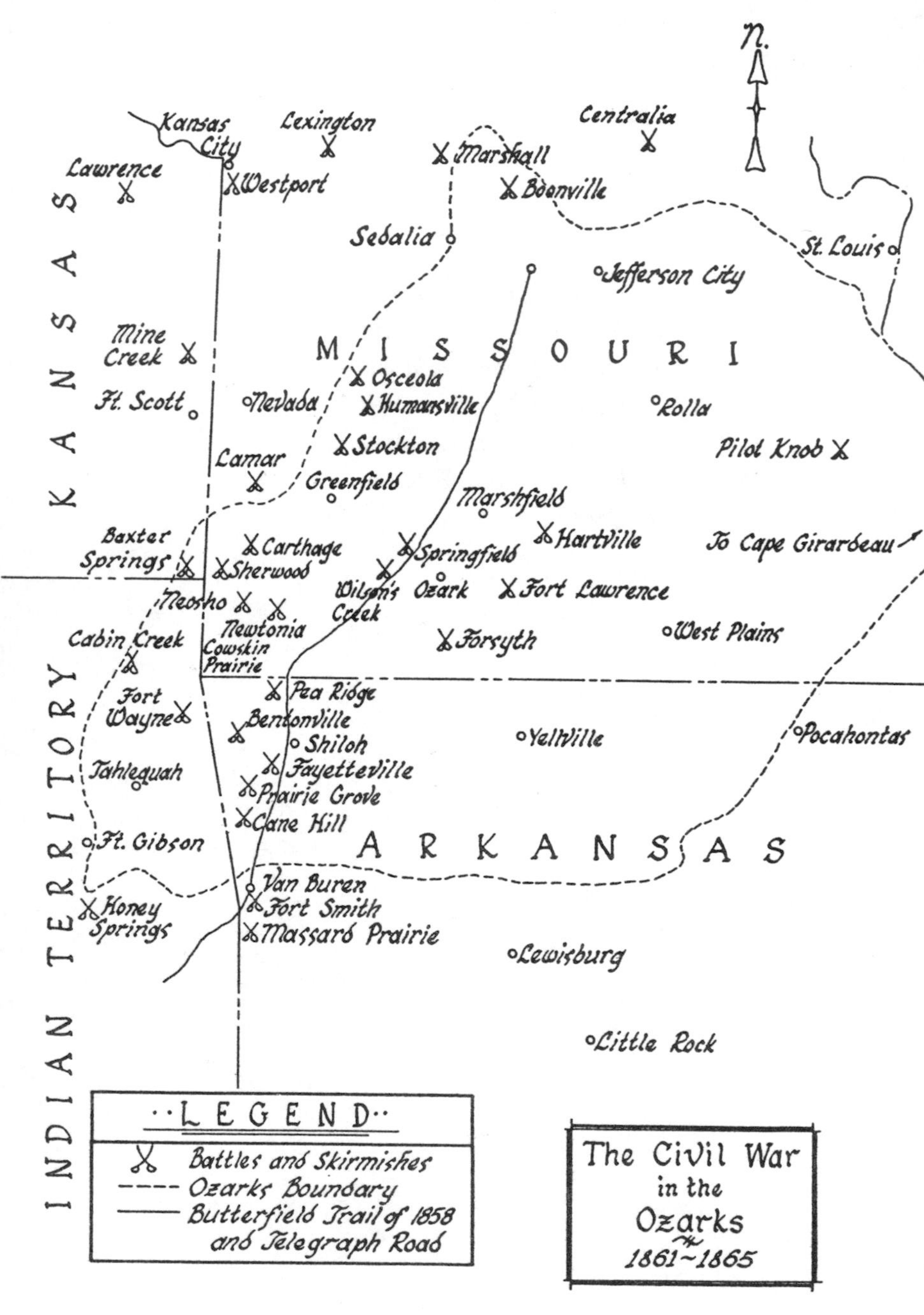
N.
Kansas City
Lexington
Centralia
Lawrence
Westport
Marshall
Boonville
Sebalia
St. Louis
Jefferson City
KANSAS
MISSOURI
Mine Creek
Osceola
Humansville
Ft. Scott
Nevada
Rolla
Stockton
Pilot Knob
Lamar
Greenfield
Marshfield
Baxter Springs
Carthage
Springfield
Hartville
To Cape Girardeau
Sherwood
Wilson's Creek
Ozark
Fort Lawrence
Neosho
Newtonia
West Plains
Cabin Creek
Cowskin Prairie
Forsyth
Pea Ridge
Fort Wayne
Bentonville
Yellville
Pocahontas
Shiloh
Tahlequah
Fayetteville
Prairie Grove
Cane Hill
Ft. Gibson
ARKANSAS
Van Buren
Honey Springs
Fort Smith
Massard Prairie
Lewisburg
Little Rock
INDIAN TERRITORY
LEGEND
Battles and Skirmishes
Ozarks Boundary
Butterfield Trail of 1858 and Telegraph Road
The Civil War in the Ozarks 1861~1865

Contents

CIVIL WAR in the Ozarks

The drums and fifers created enthusiasm among the volunteers and helped recruitment as the proud soldiers marched through the Ozarks. (A reenactment photo)

CHAPTER 1

The Winds of War 1861

It is hard to imagine today that the beautiful rolling hills of the southern Missouri and north Arkansas Ozarks were once one of the bloodiest regions in our nation's great Civil War.

Geologists tell us that these sprawling highlands of mid-America known as the Ozarks are our nation's oldest mountain range. Once the homeland of the warring Osage and other Indian tribes, early French explorers took note of the beautiful and unusually strong wood [*bois d'arc*, "bow wood"] the Indians were using to make their weapons, which flourished in abundance throughout the region. The French then began referring to the land as "*la région aux arcs*," meaning "the area of the bows." Simple phonetics over the years therefore created the word Ozark from this corruption of "*aux arcs*." Today, this tree [pronounced locally "bow dark" or "bow doc"], which still flourishes throughout the region, is often referred to as a hedgeapple tree as a result of its tendency to grow along fence rows and form a hedge. This tree produces large yellow apples in the fall which are useless and poisonous. One of the many Ozark legends created by early settlers in the region tells that this tree once produced an abundance of the most delicious fruit ever known to mankind. When Adam was enticed by Eve to eat the forbidden fruit, God turned the fruit to poison and caused thorns to grow from this once beautiful tree. From this legend of religious significance the tree is today also sometimes referred to as the devil's tree and its fruit as devil's apples.

It is therefore of little wonder that the beautiful Ozarks, named after the wood of the devil's tree, which once provided early Indian cultures with a source for their weaponry, became an early breeding ground for political conflict that would result in the Civil War.

Long before Fort Sumter was fired upon, feuding between Missouri and north Arkansas slaveholders with Kansas abolitionists had begun as early as 1855. Families along the Missouri-Kansas border country of the western Ozarks found themselves caught up in routine violence. Continual fighting between Ozark border ruffians and Kansas Jayhawkers continued for some six years before the official War Between the States began in 1861.

Those who attempted to remain neutral in the Ozarks sooner or later found themselves or their loved ones as victims of the war's violence, causing them to forsake their neutrality for either defense or vengeance. Most early Ozark settlers had originally come from Southern states and were sympathetic to the Confederacy. However, there was also a formidable number of Union sympathizers present in the region. These Union men bitterly fought their fellow neighbors throughout the Ozarks. Arkansas had seceded from the Union, yet many hill folk remained stubbornly loyal to the Federal government. The southwest tip of the Ozarks in Indian Territory (the present state of Oklahoma) brought forth some hard-riding Cherokee Rebels. The Choctaw, Chickasaw, Seminole, and Creek Tribes also spawned a zealous group of warriors on both sides. Thus the Ozarks, like the rest of the nation, had divided loyalties in the spring of 1861. Those divisions would fan the flames of war that set this beautiful region ablaze with violence for the next four years.

One of the most critical military problems west of the Mississippi River concerned the fate of Missouri. The "Border State" was disputed territory, dividing the far western

These Kansas artillerymen, veterans of the Missouri-Kansas border war which began long before the first shot was fired at Fort Sumter, proudly pose with their cannon. (Photo courtesy Civil War Museum, Carthage, Missouri)

Problems created for slaveowners in western Missouri and northwest Arkansas by Kansas abolitionists fueled the fires of war in the Ozarks. Such problems became secondary to the major issue of the right for states to challenge the Federal government in 1861. As the war in the Ozarks progressed, such original problems became simply defense, vengeance, and survival. (Photo courtesy Civil War Museum, Carthage, Missouri)

A second state convention was held in Arkansas on May 6, 1861. Although under David Walker's leadership, the Unionists succeeded in preventing the state from secession, the delegates voted 65-55 to secede at this second session. Walker then called for unanimous support to secede. Former state senator Isaac Murphy of Madison County, Arkansas, was a strong Union supporter and friend of Walker's but was one of only four who voted "no" to Walker's proposal. Such political division among state leaders over secession was common throughout the South. (Photo courtesy UALR Archives, Little Rock, Arkansas)

Confederacy from the North, and its strategic position was vital for control of the Mississippi River. The fate of Missouri was to be determined through the outcome of battles fought in the Ozark region.

By summer of 1861, Missouri had become a battlefield. The state's pro-Southern governor, Claiborne F. Jackson, and his poorly equipped militia, the Missouri State Guard, were rapidly driven from the central portion of the state by fiery Union brigadier general Nathaniel Lyon. After losing the state capital at Jefferson City, the State Guard suffered a humiliating defeat in a brief skirmish at Boonville on June 17. Led by Governor Jackson's nephew, Col. John S. Marmaduke, the Guardsmen at Boonville stood their ground long enough to get off a few shots. However, the glint of Yankee bayonets and several noisy shells from Lyon's artillery sent the inexperienced Rebel farm boys scurrying off in a frantic retreat known as the "Boonville Races."

Thus the defeated, yet still defiant, militiamen retreated south with their squirrel rifles and shotguns slung over their tired shoulders. The overall military commander of the Missouri State Guard, Maj. Gen. Sterling Price, rode toward Arkansas with a small force to solicit the aid of regular Confederate troops. Meanwhile, a detachment of Union troops in southwest Missouri had been ordered to cut off the retreat of Governor Jackson's main force. Made up of German immigrants from St. Louis, the foreign-born Yankee soldiers were well trained and disciplined although many had not yet mastered the English language. In command of this force was a European-trained military tactician and veteran of the unsuccessful German Revolution of 1848, Col. Franz Sigel.

On July 5, 1861, Sigel's "Yankee Dutch" collided with Jackson's Rebel Guardsmen at the small town of Carthage, Missouri, a prosperous community of 500 residents and the county seat of Jasper County, Missouri. Full-scale war had come to the Ozark Region. Preceding the famous Battle of

Confederate governor Claiborne F. Jackson of Missouri, the only presiding state governor in the American Civil War to personally command troops in battle. (Photo courtesy Civil War Museum, Carthage, Missouri)

Clouds of sulphurous smoke blanketed the battlefield as Confederate and Federal battle lines marched to their destiny. (A reenactment photo)

Bull Run in Virginia by more than two weeks, the Battle of Carthage made headlines in newspapers across the nation. *The New York Times* described it as, "The first serious conflict between the United States troops and the rebels."

The opposing forces encountered each other about nine miles north of town between Dry Fork and Opossum Creek. Sigel's force consisted of two regiments totalling 1,100 troops, 950 infantrymen supported by eight artillery pieces with full gun crews. Most, if not all, of Sigel's enlisted men sported simple gray uniforms and wide-brimmed hats. At this early stage of the war, "Union Blue" versus "Confederate Gray" was not yet an established color code. The Missouri State Guard troops could not be mistaken for Sigel's gray-clad "Hessians" because they had not been issued uniforms. Dressed in their everyday civilian clothing, most of the Guardsmen were ill fed and poorly armed. Some 2,000 of Jackson's 3,500 cavalrymen had no weapons. Most of his 2,000 infantrymen were armed merely with shotguns and hunting rifles they had brought from home. However, Jackson had seven artillery pieces to strengthen his amateur army of approximately 6,000 troops. He also had a competent staff, including the ranking officer on the field, Brig. Gen. James S. Rains, a former state senator.

Although Sigel was outnumbered nearly six to one, his infantry was well equipped with powerful .69-caliber military muskets. A number of his men had been formed into "rifle companies." These units carried weapons which had been rifled to accommodate the new Minié bullet, a hollow-based conical projectile, originally designed by an officer of the French Army, Capt. Claude Minié, which was more accurate than the old-fashioned round ball. Furthermore, Sigel's force was far better trained than Jackson's army. The Union commander had little respect for the ragtag Missouri State Guard with its poor battle record. With the steady nerve of a veteran soldier, he sternly surveyed Jackson's long battle line that stretched across a rising slope of open prairie for nearly a mile. Then the Yankee colonel, with a strong German accent, boldly ordered his artillery to open fire.

At approximately 8:30 A.M. on July 5, 1861, the thunderclap of a cannon salvo shattered the peace of the surrounding countryside. The Union gun batteries blasted holes in the disrupted line of militia. Yet the Missouri State Guard was tired of running. The determined Guards reformed their lines and stood their ground. As in all major combat situations during the war, both sides formed battle lines with troops shoulder to shoulder. Such battle formations seem to be suicidal by today's standards but, considering the musket and cannon weaponry of the day, such battle line formations were commonplace. With thousands of men gathered together firing muzzleloaders as rapidly as possible, it didn't take long for a battlefield to become shrouded in a thick blanket of gunsmoke. Frequently, the enemy could not be seen through the swirling, sulfureous clouds. The best chance of hitting a target under such conditions was for men to stand in line and fire a volley at the same time, thereby creating a flying wall of lead traveling in the general direction of their foe. Also the line formation helped commanders maintain control of their troops and reduced the chances of some men getting separated from their unit, becoming lost or disoriented in the infernal smoke.

Soon after Sigel's artillery went into action, Capt. Hiram Bledsoe's three-gun State Guard battery returned fire with deadly accuracy. One of Bledsoe's artillery pieces was a fine cannon which he himself had helped to capture in the Mexican War at the Battle of Sacramento in 1847. It is said to have been cast from Mexican church bells and even had its own name, "Old Sacramento." Accounts claim that whenever "Ol Sac" was fired, the big gun would produce a peculiar ringing sound that could be heard across the battlefield.

The noisy artillery duel lasted at least half an hour, churning the battlefield with chaos and bloodshed. Meanwhile the Missouri State Guard made good use of many unarmed

Union general Franz Sigel. After leading troops in battle at Carthage, Wilson's Creek, and Pea Ridge, he was promoted to major general and sent far from the Ozarks to the Eastern Theater. His military career was essentially ruined in 1864 by the famous charge of the brave young cadets of the Virginia Military Institute at the Battle of New Market in the Shenandoah Valley. (Photo courtesy Civil War Museum, Carthage, Missouri)

horsemen by sending them on a flanking movement close enough to the enemy to be seen yet far enough away not to reveal the fact they had no weapons. This was accomplished at the same time Capt. Joseph O. Shelby's Rangers and other armed cavalry units also advanced on the Union flanks. At this point, Sigel felt compelled to retreat south before he was surrounded and cut off from his supply wagons. He began an orderly withdrawal, skillfully utilizing his artillery in repeated attempts to slow the Rebel advance.

A desperate delaying action was fought at the crossing of Dry Fork Creek. Upon reaching the south bank of the stream, Sigel ordered a small but powerful rear guard to cover the withdrawal of his main force. Several companies of Union infantry, supported by an artillery battery, formed a line of battle and opened fire on the State Guard troops approaching on the opposite bank. Urging his men forward, Lt. Col. Edwin Price, son of Gen. Sterling Price, had his horse shot from under him. Meanwhile, battle-hardened Captain Bledsoe personally manned an artillery piece as many of his men were cut down by heavy fire from across the creek. After two hours of blazing action, the stubborn Yanks withdrew to join their comrades who had retreated toward town. Many, if not most, of the day's casualties fell along the muddy banks of Dry Fork Creek. The Battle of Carthage is sometimes referred to as the Battle of Dry Fork.

To protect his supply train, Sigel ordered his wagons into four columns of eight each and positioned his men around them in a European-style infantry square. This classic troop formation, used so effectively by the British at Waterloo in 1815 and at Ulundi in 1879, was a rare occurrence on American Civil War battlefields. The Battle of Carthage may have been the only action of the entire war in which the hollow infantry square was actually utilized in combat.

Another serious stand was made by the Union force at Buck Branch farther south. It was there that the Missouri State Guard cavalry nearly succeeded in trapping the

Union Col. Franz Sigel leads his German troops forward during the Battle of Carthage, Missouri. (A reenactment photo)

Germans by blocking their retreat. However, Lt. Col. Francis Hassendeubel led a rousing bayonet charge against the cavalry line, cutting an avenue of escape for Sigel's force.

The action continued with fighting at the crossing of Spring River and soon the storm of battle swirled through the streets of Carthage itself. House-to-house fighting left several buildings damaged by musket and artillery fire. Stubbornly giving way to the advancing Rebels, the Yanks had to abandon two of their supply wagons in town. The battle continued until nightfall. Darkness allowed Colonel Sigel to break contact with Governor Jackson's army and march his exhausted troops another 18 miles to safety in the town of Sarcoxie, Missouri.

It had been a long, hot battle featuring countless artillery salvos and musket volleys. Yet despite the heavy gunfire and frantic troop maneuvers, the death toll was light. While accounts of the number of casualties at the Battle of Carthage differ greatly, the most commonly accepted tally indicates 13 Union soldiers were killed and 31 wounded, 5 of whom were captured; while Jackson's militia had 35 killed, 125 wounded, and 45 captured. The brick courthouse on the town square became a hospital for the suffering casualties. A number of townspeople helped with the gory task of treating the scores of wounded soldiers there. It is said that one of those who volunteered for nursing duty was a young teenage girl named Myra Maebelle Shirley whose family owned and operated the Shirley House, a hotel and tavern in Carthage. Later in the war, after her brother Bud Shirley was killed by Union troops in a guerrilla skirmish near Sarcoxie, young Myra Maebelle fled to Texas with the rest of her family to settle in Scyene where John Shirley once again opened a hotel and tavern. Myra Maebelle later became the notorious Belle Starr.

The Battle of Carthage lifted the morale of the Missouri State Guard and other Southern sympathizers in the region. Jackson's men had won a full-scale battle against well-trained

Myra Maebelle Shirley, the daughter of John Shirley, who operated the Shirley House Hotel and Tavern in Carthage, Missouri, was age 13 when the Civil War in the Ozarks began in 1861. The Shirley Tavern was a popular place for heated political discussions and young Belle became an activist for the Confederate cause at an early age. Her brother John Allison ("Bud") Shirley joined the Confederate Army. Learning of Union movements in the region, young Belle would often carry such information to Confederate camps. While dining at a Mrs. Stewart's home near Sarcoxie, Missouri, with several Confederate companions, Ed Shirley was killed when the group was attacked by a Union party. Young Belle and her mother went to Sarcoxie to claim the body a short time before the Shirley family decided to leave Missouri for Texas. No doubt the death of her beloved brother and the bitterness caused within her as a result of the Civil War greatly contributed to Belle Shirley eventually becoming the infamous Belle Starr, the Outlaw Queen. Following the War, many former Quantrill guerrillas drifted into Texas to often visit Shirley's Tavern there where Belle renewed her Missouri admiration for such men as Jesse and Frank James, the Youngers, and Jim Reed, who became her first husband. (Photo courtesy Robert Hutton family)

A dime-novel illustration of the Union attack on Mrs. Stuart's home near Sarcoxie, Missouri, in which John Allison ("Bud") Shirley, Belle Starr's brother, was killed. (Photo courtesy Civil War Museum, Carthage, Missouri)

Union troops and proved themselves to be a serious fighting force. The entire nature of the war in Missouri changed after the fierce encounter at Dry Fork.

On July 6, Maj. Gen. Sterling Price, returning from Arkansas with Confederate reinforcements, linked up with Governor Jackson three miles south of Carthage. General Price was accompanied by Brig. Gen. Benjamin McCulloch in command of a force of Confederate regulars from Texas and Louisiana, and Brig. Gen. N. Bart Pearce, in command of a force of Arkansas state troops. On their march north toward Carthage, the reinforcements had achieved another victory on the fateful day of July 5, 1861. Two battalions of Southern troops entered Neosho, Missouri, where Sigel had left nearly 100 of his men to secure the town. The totally surprised Germans offered no resistance and were easily captured along with 150 arms and seven wagonloads of supplies.

Upon learning that the Missouri State Guard had whipped Sigel's main force, McCulloch and Pearce returned to Arkansas with their troops. Sterling Price, a former governor of Missouri and Mexican War general, planned his strategy with Governor Jackson. The Guardsmen anxiously awaited the next move by their 51-year-old leader whom they fondly referred to as "Old Pap." Swinging his 250 pounds into the saddle, Price led his army to a spot known as "Cowskin Prairie" where he established a training camp for the State Guard. The camp was located in the southwest corner of Missouri, three miles north of the Arkansas border and three miles east of Indian Territory.

Meanwhile, General Lyon had entered Springfield with a force of nearly 6,000 Union troops. Lyon was a tough little red-bearded veteran of Indian campaigns in the West. The tireless Union commander set about to gather information concerning the strength and location of the Rebel army. While planning his campaign against Price's troops, Lyon received various pieces of information and misinformation concerning other nearby pockets of armed resistance to

Federal authority. The most exaggerated of these scouting reports concerned the town of Forsyth, Missouri, a Rebel supply base and county seat of Taney County situated southeast of Springfield. Lyon responded to these reports by ordering a detachment of 1,200 troops to take the town from the Rebels. In command of the expedition was an Irish immigrant who had lost an arm in the Mexican War. Thomas Sweeny held a dual rank as both a regular army captain and a brigadier general of volunteers.

Sweeny's men left Springfield about noon on Saturday, July 20, and the next day arrived in the village of Ozark, Missouri. It was there that the Irishman's troops took whatever they wanted, including an entire wagonload of whiskey, which they soon consumed. By July 22, they were on the outskirts of Forsyth. Sweeny ordered his cavalry, two companies of regulars, and one loosely disciplined group of Kansans, to launch the assault. Capt. David Stanley led a colorful charge through the streets and up a steep hill east of town, easily driving the meager force of about 150 local Rebel defenders before them. During the attack, some of the Kansas cavalrymen dismounted and began looting the courthouse. To the misfortune of the Kansans, the Union artillery commander misunderstood an order by Sweeny and began shelling the building. The terrified troopers scurried from the courthouse like rats from a burning barn.

The raid on Forsyth cost no Union lives and only two soldiers were wounded. Sweeny reported that eight or ten Rebels were killed and several times that many were wounded. Other than the capture of a good supply of clothing and footwear intended for Price's men, the Forsyth expedition accomplished very little. It was merely an adventurous little outing for Sweeny and his men featuring free whiskey and the chance to shoot up a town.

Meanwhile, General Price had decided it was time for his troops to leave Cowskin Prairie and undertake the task of making Missouri free from Federal rule. On July 25 he

Brig. Gen. Sterling Price, prior to 1861, had served three terms in the U.S. Congress and four years as governor of the state of Missouri. Like most Missourians, he favored remaining in the Union, but events forced him to take sides. Price chose the South and was appointed commander of the Missouri State Guard. "Old Pap," as the some 7,000 men in his force affectionately called him, along with Brig. Gen. Ben McCulloch, was determined to drive the Union Army out of Missouri. (Photo courtesy the Arkansas History Commission, Little Rock, Arkansas)

Brig. Gen. James McIntosh was awarded his rank by Gen. Ben McCulloch on the battlefield at Wilson's Creek. Praising McIntosh for his leadership, McCulloch commented, "he was everywhere the balls flew the thickest," and gave McIntosh command of the Confederate cavalry. At the Battle of Pea Ridge, McIntosh was killed on March 7, 1862, moments after McCulloch also went down. (Photo courtesy UALR Archives, Little Rock, Arkansas)

marched his army east across the Ozark countryside to Cassville, Missouri. There Brig. Gen. J. H. McBride with his command of 700 state troops from the Ozark hills joined Price. McBride's hillbilly soldiers knew nothing of military manners and drill, but they were tough as nails and crack shots with their hunting rifles. On July 29, Generals McCulloch and Pearce with their commands united with the Missourians at their Cassville camp, added 5,700 more men to the swelling Rebel force. On August 1, over 13,000 Southerners marched out of Cassville to do battle with the Federal troops. At this point the Rebel army had no overall commander. Price and McCulloch retained their individual commands while attempting to cooperate with each other on strategic matters.

In Springfield, General Lyon had telegraphed St. Louis requesting reinforcements from his superior, Maj. Gen. John C. Frémont, commander of the Department of the West. Although no reinforcements had arrived, he determined to attempt a foray against the Rebels without the extra troops. He did not yet know for sure that Price had linked up with McCulloch. The fearless Lyon marched from Springfield on August 1. His vanguard consisted of about 900 men, four companies of infantry, an artillery battery, and Captain Stanley's cavalry. The next day this force encountered the Rebel vanguard consisting of 500 men from the Missouri State Guard cavalry under command of Gen. James Rains. A lively skirmish ensued near Dug Spring. Rains' cavalry was embarrassingly put to flight with just one killed and five wounded. The Federals, with four dead and six wounded, pressed on until the next day, August 3, when Lyon realized what a precarious situation he was in. Arriving back in Springfield on August 5, Lyon was well aware of McCulloch's presence and that his own position in southwest Missouri was untenable without reinforcements from Frémont.

Since joining together in Cassville, it had been obvious to Price, McCulloch, and Pearce that someone needed to be in overall command. Two days after the skirmish at Dug Spring,

General McCulloch assumed this position through a consensus of the leaders. This was thought to be best since his general's commission was granted by the central government of the Confederacy while Price and Pearce were only state militia officers. In his time, McCulloch was very well known for his frontier exploits. First gaining a reputation as a top-notch bear hunter and Indian fighter, he later journeyed to Texas with Davy Crockett. He fought with distinction under Sam Houston at the Battle of San Jacinto, and when the United States declared war on Mexico, McCulloch led a unit of Texas Rangers in the conflict. He headed for California during the gold rush of 1849 and there became sheriff of Sacramento. At the outbreak of hostilities in 1861, McCulloch organized a regiment of Texas cavalry and, as its colonel, accepted the surrender of all Federal military posts and U.S. government property in the state of Texas. Following this achievement, President Jefferson Davis granted him a general's commission. Now at 50 years of age, he was in command of an army of over 13,000 men and had reached the pinnacle of his career as a soldier of fortune.

Taking a route up the Telegraph Road[1], McCulloch's army slowly neared Springfield. According to McCulloch's official report, his total effective force, not counting about 2,000 unarmed Missouri State Guardsmen, was 5,300 infantry, 6,000 cavalry, and 15 pieces of artillery. This force included Missourians, Arkansans, Texans, Louisianians, and some half-breeds and full-bloods from Indian Territory. The Union troops in Springfield numbered only about 6,400 fully armed men and 18 pieces of artillery. This force included Unionist Missourians, many of whom were German immigrants, Kansans, Iowa volunteers, and U.S. Army regulars.

---

1. A telegraph line was raised from St. Louis to Ft. Smith in 1858 along a stretch of road that subsequently became known as the Telegraph Road or Wire Road. This road through the Ozarks was also used by the Butterfield Overland mail coaches from 1858 to 1862.

By August 6, McCulloch's force was encamped 10 miles southwest of Springfield along Wilson's Creek. After a prolonged delay, the Rebels prepared for action. A march was to be made on the town the night of August 9, but it rained. Many of McCulloch's troops had only untreated canvas bags or merely their trouser pockets in which to keep their paper cartridges. Since wet gunpowder makes for poor firepower, the march was canceled.

Meanwhile, Lyon was tired of sitting in Springfield and he could not bear the thought of an inglorious retreat north. He too planned to march against his foe on that same rainy night! With regulation leather cartridge boxes to keep their powder dry, the Federals set out from Springfield, leaving 1,000 troops behind to guard the supplies and hold the town. By 5:00 A.M. the soggy Yanks had reached their destination and were deployed according to an audacious battle plan designed by Col. Franz Sigel and approved by General Lyon. Lyon, with the main body of troops, prepared to strike the Rebels from the north while Sigel, with 1,200 troops, had swung wide to the south to attack the opposite end of the sprawling camp. The Union force of approximately 5,400 was split in two in the presence of an enemy force more than twice as strong! Yet the element of surprise gave the Yanks initial success. Union artillery shells exploded mercilessly within the Southern camps, throwing debris high into the air. Men scrambled desperately for their weapons as charred tent flaps and twisted cooking gear rained down upon them. Fireballs soon erupted among the numerous Confederate supply wagons. Terrified mule teams, many still hitched to blazing wagons, raced frantically across the field. Around 6:00 A.M. both Lyon and Sigel were fully engaged in combat with their foes and, steadily advancing, drove the surprised Southerners before them.

But the surprise was soon over. From high ground to the east, William E. Woodruff's artillery battery from Pulaski County, Arkansas, opened fire on Lyon's advancing troops.

A typical Confederate infantry advance across hundreds of Ozark battlefields. (A reenactment photo)

Woodruff's four bronze guns halted the Union general's line of battle on a rise of land to be known henceforth as "Bloody Hill." General Price quickly rallied his men and launched a furious counterattack. Soon the familiar ringing echo of Captain Bledsoe's "Old Sacramento" joined the growing storm of artillery thunder. To the south, General McCulloch brought a halt to Sigel's advance and sent the Gray-clad 3rd Louisiana Infantry forward. Sigel mistook them for the 1st Iowa Volunteers, a Union regiment that also wore gray uniforms. The Louisiana troops were too close before the mistake was realized and Sigel's force was badly mauled. Unable to recover from the onslaught, his men were completely routed by McCulloch's continued assault upon their line. Sigel's troops fled, abandoning five artillery pieces. Their colonel had little choice but to flee or face capture. Accompanied by an aide, Sigel galloped off to Springfield. He would live to fight another day.

On Bloody Hill, General Lyon fought on. Never having received word of Sigel's defeat, the stubborn Connecticut Yankee was now taking on the entire Rebel army alone with his small force. Around 9:00 A.M. he had to bring up his reserves to repel the steady Rebel assaults. Having been wounded twice and with one horse already shot from under him, Lyon continued to remain in the midst of the heavy action. At approximately 9:30 A.M. General Lyon was leading a charge when a musket ball tore into his chest. Slipping from his saddle into the arms of his aide, Pvt. Edward Lehman, his last words were simply, "Lehman, I am killed."

So many high-ranking officers had become casualties by the time of Lyon's death that the command of the Federal force fell upon the shoulders of a major. Samuel Sturgis, who had led a force of Federal troops from Fort Levenworth, Kansas, to join Lyon's command, continued the fight until 11:30 A.M. when he finally ordered a withdrawal. The Rebels had won. The Yanks retreated to Springfield and then withdrew to Rolla, Missouri.

Thus the Union's first campaign to drive the Secessionist forces from Missouri ended abruptly with the death of Lyon, the first Union general in the Civil War to be killed in action. The Battle of Wilson's Creek, called Oak Hills by the Confederates, subdued for a brief time the strength of the Federal military effort in Missouri. The casualties were staggering for only a six-hour battle, with 1,317 Federals and 1,222 Southerners killed, wounded, or missing. Twenty-five percent of all the men who fought on Bloody Hill that day were casualties.

Following their victory, Price advanced north while McCulloch and Pearce merely returned to Arkansas. In an attempt to retake the entire state, Price reached the Missouri River in late August with a force swollen by new recruits. With approximately 10,000 men he advanced on the strategic Union stronghold at Lexington where 3,000 Union troops under Col. James Mulligan were dug in on high ground. After a dramatic siege, the Yankees surrendered on September 20 and gave Price his most glorious victory of the war.

During Price's advance north, a small force of Union troops had followed a safe distance behind the State Guard. This force was no ordinary group of Yanks. A United States senator from Kansas had returned to his home state in the summer of 1861 with a burning desire to revive his pre-war activity of leading Kansans against Missourians. James H. Lane was to retain his Senate seat while occasionally rampaging through Missouri as a commander of Kansas troops. Known as the "Grim Chieftain," he organized and led "Lane's Brigade" during Price's Lexington campaign. Composed of Kansas infantry and cavalry, this force was in fact a ruthless band of Jayhawkers wearing Union uniforms. Lane's route of pillage and plunder that September brought him to the town of Osceola, Missouri. This community of 2,000 was the county seat of St. Clair County and had strong Southern sympathies. It was here on September 22 that Lane and his men firmly established their criminal reputation.

Brig. Gen. Nathaniel Lyon was the first Union general killed in action during the Civil War. During a hasty retreat from the Battle of Wilson's Creek, Lyon's body was mistakenly left behind on the battlefield. (Photo courtesy Civil War Museum, Carthage, Missouri)

When the Kansans found a cache of Rebel military supplies in the town, their "Chieftain" decided to wipe Osceola from the map. But first Osceola was stripped of all its valuable goods which were loaded into wagons hastily commandeered from the townspeople. Then nine citizens were given a farcical trial and shot. There was also an apparent attempt by Lane's men to consume all the liquor in town, of which there was a very good supply. Finally the raiders brought their frenzy of pillage, murder, and drunkenness to a close by burning the town. When the smoke cleared, only three buildings remained standing, and Lane's brigade was homeward bound to Lawrence, Kansas.

Meanwhile, following Price's victory at Lexington, General Frémont finally left his lavish St. Louis headquarters and took to the field under a hail of sharp criticism for his inactivity. Like McCulloch, Frémont was also a legend in his own time, but even more so. As a young Army officer, he had led government exploration expeditions in the West. With Kit Carson as his chief scout, Frémont discovered routes to be used by wagon trains carrying settlers beyond the Rocky Mountains. Dubbed "The Pathfinder" for his achievements, this famous Western explorer also played a dramatic role in wresting California from Mexican rule. In the 1850s, Frémont embraced the Abolitionist cause and became the first Republican candidate for president of the United States in 1856. At the outbreak of hostilities in 1861, the North expected great things from this Western hero. Unfortunately, Frémont's days of glory were behind him. The Union defeats at both Wilson's Creek and Lexington were blamed on him for his failure to reinforce Lyon and Mulligan in their hours of need. Actually, he had in fact ordered reinforcements in both cases, but failures by a number of his field officers prevented their arrival. Attempting to save his reputation, Frémont personally led an army of 20,000 troops in pursuit of Price's State Guards, trailing the illusive Rebels back to southwest Missouri.

John C. Frémont, the famous Western scout and explorer, served the Union as a major general, commanding the Department of the West. (Photo courtesy Civil War Museum, Carthage, Missouri)

In the vanguard of Frémont's army as it neared Springfield on October 24 were two companies of scouts and a large detachment of the general's "Body Guard," a fancy unit consisting of three companies of well-equipped and colorfully uniformed cavalrymen. Preparing to ambush the approaching Yanks was an inexperienced band of approximately 1,000 local Rebel militiamen under the command of Col. Julian Frazier.

Colonel Frazier concealed a strong force in the woods along both sides of a road that led to his camp on the western outskirts of town. Silently they waited, hoping the approaching Federals would gallop down the lane in an assault on the camp. Soon the Blue-coated horsemen arrived on the scene and their Hungarian commander, Maj. Charles Zagonyi, ordered his fancy cavalrymen forward to charge the Rebel camp by way of the road. The cocky troopers were soon greeted with a deadly storm of Rebel lead that sent men and horses crashing to the ground in terrible tangled masses. Yet amazingly the cavalrymen regrouped under cover of a hill, proving themselves to be true soldiers. Zagonyi led a second charge, this time directly into the Rebel positions, and totally routed Frazier's troops. The scattered Rebels were pursued through the streets of Springfield and the surrounding countryside. Zagonyi later estimated the defeated militiamen's casualties at more than 100.

After the action died down, the troopers assembled in the town square where some pro-Union citizens warmly greeted them and Union prisoners were freed from the jail. Then, fearing a counterattack, Zagonyi confiscated more than $4,000 in gold from the local bank and led his men out of Springfield to rejoin Frémont's main force.

At the cost of 53 casualties among the Body Guards and 31 among the scouts, the bold Zagonyi had achieved a meaningless little victory in the only action to be fought in Frémont's expedition to southwest Missouri. Entering Springfield a few days later, Frémont established his headquarters there only to be notified soon afterward of his relief from command. Under instructions from his superiors, the new commander, Maj. Gen. David Hunter, pulled all his troops back north for the winter. One column under Brig. Gen. John Pope was ordered to Sedalia, while another column under Brig. Gen. Franz Sigel was ordered to Rolla. The Kansas troops under Brig. Gen. Samuel Sturgis and Sen. James Lane were ordered back to their own state.

Meanwhile, on October 28, 1861, in the town of Neosho, Missouri, Secessionist legislators under Governor Jackson voted for Missouri to leave the Union and join the Confederacy. A great celebration took place with Price's artillerymen firing their guns to salute the event. To these men, it was Independence Day. The Confederate Congress in Richmond, Virginia, officially accepted Missouri as the 12th state of the Confederacy on November 28, and measures were taken to eventually transfer the Missouri State Guard into the regular Confederate States Army. The year of 1861 was drawing to a close, and the majority of the Ozarks remained under Southern control. Yet the fight had just begun.

CHAPTER 2

Full-Scale War
1862

Wintering at Springfield, Price's troops found their training for the oncoming spring campaign rudely interrupted. It was early February of 1862 and Brig. Gen. Samuel R. Curtis, newly appointed commander of the Federal District of Southwest Missouri, was marching nearly 12,000 Union troops in Price's direction. A serious, grandfatherly man with an impressive background, Curtis was a West Point graduate, Mexican War veteran, lawyer, civil engineer, and former U.S. Congressman. But most importantly, Curtis was destined to be remembered by posterity as the general who regained Missouri for the Union in one single, decisive battle.

Price dared not risk a confrontation alone against the superior numbers of Union troops. On February 12, he began marching his army toward Arkansas to link up with General McCulloch. His retreat soon became a race for life with Curtis' advance units occasionally skirmishing with the Confederate rear guard. Upon crossing the state line, Price still had the relentless Curtis on his tail. The new Federal commander was not at all shy of invading Arkansas.

Together once again, Price and McCulloch assessed the situation and decided against giving battle immediately. They chose to withdraw south from the town of Fayetteville, Arkansas, where much of McCulloch's army had been quartered since the Battle of Wilson's Creek. This decision did not help

Union general Samuel Curtis, a West Pointer, left the military to pursue an engineering profession before the Civil War. He also was elected to the United States Congress. On Christmas Day, 1861, he assumed command of the Union Army in the Southwest. Moving his forces southward from his Rolla, Missouri, headquarters, he was the decisive victor at the Battle of Pea Ridge in Arkansas and the Battle of Westport, Missouri, in 1864 during Sterling Price's raid. (Photo courtesy State Historical Society of Missouri, Columbia)

the morale of the troops but the feeling was minor compared to the spirit of the local populace after what occurred on February 22, the day of the Confederate evacuation. Believing everything left behind would be destroyed or carried away by the approaching Yanks, the town's business district was totally plundered by Confederate troops and a few frenzied citizens. That evening as the last of the soldiers left Fayetteville, the 3rd Louisiana Regiment raced through the downtown district hurling fiery torches left and right. Soon the entire business district was ablaze. The flaming Female Seminary, full of ammunition, exploded in a blinding flash, throwing fiery debris over a wide area. Arkansas College caught on fire, the town's Episcopal church burned to the ground, and a number of private homes were engulfed by flames. Fayetteville had been shamefully pillaged and burned, not by the enemy but by Confederate troops that had been stationed there for half a year.

In the meantime, the Confederate government, aware of tense incidents of discord between Price and McCulloch, appointed a general as overall commander of their combined forces. Maj. Gen. Earl Van Dorn was transferred west to take personal charge of the forces which became known as the Army of the West. Van Dorn was a dashing and reckless Southern cavalier with a strong passion for guns and women. His fondness for the ladies eventually led to his own untimely death when he was shot by a jealous husband in 1863.

Assuming command on March 3, General Van Dorn lost no time in making his move against Curtis' advancing force. The day after his arrival, Van Dorn marched his troops northward out of the Boston Mountains to do battle with the Union invaders of Arkansas. Advancing up the valley of Little Sugar Creek near Bentonville, Arkansas, Van Dorn's tired force arrived at Confederate Camp Stephens on the evening of March 6.

Just four miles southwest of the camp, approximately 10,500 Yanks were dug in on high bluffs overlooking the

Confederate Maj. Gen. Earl Van Dorn, who ran out of ammunition at the Battle of Pea Ridge, Arkansas, which sealed the fate of the Confederacy in the Ozarks.

valley where Curtis had calculated the Rebels would advance. Van Dorn, aware of the strong Federal entrenchments, decided to attack his foe from the rear. Flanking Curtis' position during the night, Van Dorn hoped not only to surprise the Federals, but also to gain control of Telegraph Road, the main north-south route and Curtis' communication and supply lines.

Van Dorn's advance force, 6,200 troops under General Price, failed to reach its attack position by daylight as planned. It was not until 8:00 A.M. that Price arrived at his position and even then, McCulloch's 10,000 troops were still three miles away. Van Dorn chose not to delay any longer but rather to launch a two-phased attack with simultaneous assaults upon the Federals' right and left. However, the element of surprise was already lost and Curtis had turned his men about and marched most of them away from their fortified positions to meet the enemy approaching from the north.

At approximately 10:00 A.M. the Union army collided with Van Dorn's forces at two separate areas of battle. One was near an inn known as Elkhorn Tavern, and the other two miles away on the other side of Round Top Mountain near a village called Leetown. At Elkhorn Tavern, General Price slowly pushed back Col. Eugene Carr's outnumbered Federals. The Yanks fought stubbornly throughout the day. Finally at dusk they were forced to withdraw in the face of superior numbers, but the Rebel advance had been delayed, buying valuable time for Curtis to reinforce his positions. Early in the day's battle at the Tavern, Confederate brigadier general William Slack, a Missouri veteran of the battles at Carthage and Wilson's Creek, fell with a grievous mortal wound. He would not be the last of Van Dorn's general officers to fall in battle that day.

On the other side of Round Top Mountain just north of Leetown, Gen. Ben McCulloch's troops were in a hot fight with their Blue-coated foes. The colorful Indian brigade of Brig. Gen. Albert Pike brought an early success to Confederate

The Battle of Pea Ridge in northwest Arkansas was one of the most important and largest battles fought west of the Mississippi River. Since the battle took place near the Elkhorn Tavern along the Butterfield Overland Trail, this conflict, which was to determine the fate of Missouri, is sometimes referred to as the Battle of Elkhorn Tavern. Now restored at Pea Ridge National Military Park, the structure served as a Butterfield stage station from 1858 to 1861 and as a hospital during the Battle of Pea Ridge. (Author's photo)

Hundreds of casualties covered Ozark battlefields after conflicts in the region. (A reenactment photo)

Confederate Brig. Gen. William Slack, a Missouri veteran of the battles of Carthage and Wilson's Creek, who fell mortally wounded at the Battle of Pea Ridge, Arkansas. (Photo courtesy Civil War Museum, Carthage, Missouri)

efforts in this area. Early in the war, the Confederacy had solicited the aid of various tribes within Indian Territory and sealed a number of treaties with their chiefs. This resulted in the forming of strong Indian units through General Pike's efforts to gain support for the Confederacy throughout Indian Territory. Col. Stand Watie's regiment of Cherokee Mounted Rifles was perhaps the best and certainly the most famous of the Indian units. Watie, a Cherokee himself, would later gain the distinction of being the only Native American in the Civil War to rise to the rank of brigadier general.

With the help of a detachment of Brig. Gen. James McIntosh's Texas cavalry, Pike's Indians, including Watie's men, captured three Federal artillery pieces. But when the Yanks began shelling the captured battery, Pike's long-haired warriors ran to the cover of nearby woods, abandoning their newly acquired "shooting wagons." Advancing Union troops reported the discovery of a number of scalped casualties on this portion of the battlefield, which caused a furor of outrage in the North over the conduct of the Indian forces.

Meanwhile, McCulloch joined McIntosh's cavalry in a blazing advance against the Union troops of Col. Peter Osterhaus. Later, during a lull in the day's action, the legendary Texan emerged from the woods into a clearing to better survey the field. A sharpshooter's bullet dropped him from the saddle and suddenly Gen. Ben McCulloch was dead. McIntosh assumed command of McCulloch's troops only to be shot dead himself 15 minutes later. To top off the day's Confederate disasters, Col. Louis Hébert's Louisiana troops were mauled by a Union counterattack that ended with a Rebel defeat at Leetown and the capture of Hébert. As dusk faded into night, both sides prepared to renew the bloody contest in the morning.

The second day the battle raged at Elkhorn Tavern where the Yanks had lost ground the day before. Brig. Gen. Franz Sigel, second to Curtis in command, skillfully directed his artillery against Confederate positions near the base of the

Brig. Gen. Albert Pike, the famous Arkansas educator, was responsible for recruiting Native Americans to support the Confederacy. Pike led the Indian forces in the Battle of Pea Ridge. (Photo courtesy Civil War Museum, Carthage, Missouri)

Confederate general Ben McCulloch, the Texas frontiersman who became the victor of the Battle of Wilson's Creek, Missouri, in 1861 only to die in battle at Pea Ridge, Arkansas, the following year. (Photo courtesy Civil War Museum, Carthage, Missouri)

imposing land mass known as Pea Ridge. The Rebel artillery was running low on ammunition and could not keep pace with the terrible tempo of the battle. Braving enemy fire, 19-year-old Confederate captain Churchill Clark, grandson of the famous explorer William Clark, boldly directed his artillery battery from horseback near Elkhorn Tavern. Suddenly he pitched backward from the saddle, decapitated by a Union cannon ball.

With his wounded arm in a sling, General Price rallied the Confederate ranks for a final stand as their supply of ammunition ran low. Van Dorn, acutely aware of the critical ammunition shortage, anxiously awaited the arrival of his supply train which he had left behind at Camp Stephens. The supply wagons had to be brought around the enemy force over 12 miles of rough roads to reach Van Dorn. The priceless ammunition never reached the desperate Southern army. A quirk command by an unknown subordinate officer sent the wagons lumbering off in the wrong direction just before they reached the Confederate lines. By 10:00 A.M. Van Dorn had ordered a general retreat. He successfully deceived the Federals with a fighting force near the Tavern long enough to march his main body of troops from the field. By noon the battle was over. Incredibly, the Yanks chose the wrong road on which to pursue their vanquished foes, and the Southern army was allowed to escape south over the Boston Mountains to Van Buren, Arkansas.

Casualties at the Battle of Pea Ridge, also known as the Battle of Elkhorn Tavern, totalled nearly the same on both sides. The Union army suffered 203 killed, 980 wounded, and 201 missing in action, and the Confederates reported their losses as 1,000 killed and wounded and 300 captured. Time would show this battle to be the most decisive Federal victory west of the Mississippi River.

After the battle, most of the regular troops of both sides marched out of the Ozarks. Van Dorn's Army of the West was transferred east of the Mississippi. Governor Jackson of

Sgt. Charles S. Squires, Company G, 37th Illinois Infantry, was part of the Second Brigade, Third Division, that reinforced Osterhaus in the desperate fight with McCulloch at the Battle of Pea Ridge. The regiment lost 133 men in the battle. (Photo courtesy Western Historical Collection, University of Oklahoma)

Lt. Col. Robert McCulloch, a pro-slavery Democrat, was one of the first to raise a company for the Missouri State Guard and fought at the Battle of Wilson's Creek. After the Confederate loss at Pea Ridge, many Missourians left the service, but McCulloch stayed and told Gen. Sterling Price that he would remain "to help drive the enemy from our soil." (Photo courtesy the Missouri State Historical Society)

Missouri and Gov. Henry Rector of Arkansas were both furious over this apparent abandonment of their states by the Confederacy. Many Missouri troops were mustered into the regular Confederate States Army, forming the renowned First and Second Missouri Brigades. The Old Missouri State Guard was dissolved. Price himself resigned from it in order to accept a regular Confederate commission as major general. Tragically, few of Price's brave men who joined the regular Confederate Army were ever to see Missouri again. Most were to be casualties in the monumental struggle east of the Mississippi River.

Yet back in the Ozarks, the war was not over. There still remained a hard-core nucleus of Rebels in the region to challenge the limited number of Union troops that remained behind to guard their newly won territory. Many former State Guardsmen chose to remain in Missouri. Guerrillas and small, fast-moving detachments of Confederate cavalry kept the war hot for Yanks in the region as they preyed on Federal camps, patrols, and supply trains.

The growing number of Rebel partisans, or "bushwhackers" as they were often called, and the frequency of their devastating raids, prompted Union major general Henry Halleck, commander of the Department of the West, to issue "Order Number Two" on March 13, 1862. The order labeled all guerrillas as outlaws and required that they be executed upon capture. The guerrillas responded likewise, rarely taking prisoners. It made no difference to the Federals that on April 21, 1862, the Confederate Congress passed the Confederate Partisan Ranger Act which recognized Southern guerrilla bands as legitimate military groups with official officers. The extermination policy continued to be practiced for the remainder of the war, giving an especially vicious and desperate nature to all clashes between Confederate guerrillas and Union troops in the Ozark region.

A dramatic new turn of events changed the military situation in the Ozarks during the summer of 1862 when Maj.

Pvt. William Holcomb, son of a Northwest Arkansas minister, who founded the city of Shiloh (now Springdale), enlisted in the Confederate Army on November 1, 1861. He served in Company G, 15th Arkansas Infantry, which was a part of Gen. Ben McCulloch's forces. His regiment was forced to retreat during the Battle of Pea Ridge in which Holcomb was wounded. (Photo courtesy Washington County Historical Society, Fayetteville, Arkansas)

David Walker of Fayetteville, Arkansas, had been a member of the Arkansas constitutional convention in 1836 and helped prepare the state's constitution. He also served as a supreme court judge in the state. Walker was the most popular Unionist delegate to the March 4, 1861, convention in Arkansas, which was to decide whether the state should secede from the Union. His statement, "When I look at the blessings the Union has conferred on us, I feel like it would be almost sacrilege to even think of seeing it dissolved," helped defeat the resolution to secede from the Union by a vote of 39 to 35. (Photo courtesy UALR Archives, Little Rock, Arkansas)

Capt. Jacob Wythe Walker, son of the prominent Unionist judge David Walker of Fayetteville, Arkansas, served with the 34th Arkansas Regiment. He was mortally wounded at the Battle of Jenkins' Ferry, Arkansas, and died on May 21, 1864. (Photo courtesy Washington County Historical Society, Fayetteville, Arkansas)

Gen. Thomas C. Hindman raised a new Confederate army in Arkansas through the use of forced conscription. By September, the renewed strength of the Confederate military was beginning to show and the possession of southwest Missouri was once again to be briefly challenged.

By September 28, approximately 4,000 Confederate troops with six artillery pieces were encamped in and around the village of Newtonia, Missouri. Gen. Samuel Curtis, the newly appointed department commander, was greatly alarmed by this Rebel show of strength. Under his orders, Brig. Gen. John M. Schofield, district commander, gathered all available Federal forces in the area to once again drive the Confederates from the state.

On September 29, approximately 6,000 Union troops with 18 pieces of artillery were encamped 12 miles north of Newtonia at the town of Sarcoxie. This force was made up of German immigrants, Wisconsin volunteers, Kansas troops, and Federal Indian units. Like the Confederates, the Federals had also recruited Indians to beef up their forces out West in the Trans-Mississippi Theater. The Union commander, Brig. Gen. Frederick Salomon, was under orders not to bring on any battle until other converging Federal columns reached the area. Yet Col. Edward Lynde was dispatched from Salomon's camp with 150 cavalry troops and two howitzers to probe the Confederate position at Newtonia. Lynde's men briefly skirmished with a group of Rebels on the 29th before withdrawing. On the morning of September 30, Lynde joined another force from the Sarcoxie camp under Colonel Jacobi consisting of several companies of Wisconsin infantry, Kansas cavalry, Indian troops, and three cannons. Apparently unaware of the seriously large numbers of additional Confederates encamped within striking distance, Lynde and Jacobi attacked the Southerners at Newtonia and by 7:00 A.M. the battle had grown to major proportions.

Col. Douglas Cooper, who had replaced Gen. Albert Pike as commander of Confederate Indian troops, took overall command of the various Southern units which rallied to the defense of Newtonia, including Col. Jo Shelby's "Iron Brigade" of hard-riding cavalry. The outnumbered Federal forces had much more than they had bargained for and when Colonel Cooper's Choctaw and Chickasaw warriors galloped through the town in a howling charge, the Blue line broke to pieces. Pursued for approximately six miles, the surviving Yanks met General Salomon that afternoon advancing with his main force. Rallying the broken columns, Salomon threw the full weight of his entire force against Cooper but large numbers of his Kansas and Indian troops gave way toward evening and he was forced to retreat back to Sarcoxie in the darkness. The Union had suffered 50 killed, 80 wounded, and 115 missing that day. The victorious Confederates had only 12 killed, 63 wounded, and 3 missing.

However, the Battle of Newtonia was a hollow victory for the Southerners for by October 3, General Schofield had accumulated 18,000 troops and 52 pieces of artillery in the Newtonia area. The Yanks entered the town on October 4 and most of the Confederates fled to Arkansas where General Hindman's army was preparing for action. Once again the Missouri Ozarks was left in Federal hands.

Cooper's Choctaws and Chickasaws, joined by Stand Watie's Cherokees, fled back to Indian Territory with a detachment of the Federal force in pursuit. In command of the column of Union troops was a tough little Kansas abolitionist who had practiced medicine before the war, Brig. Gen. James G. Blunt. The Yanks overtook the Rebel warriors on October 22 at old Fort Wayne along the Arkansas and Indian Territory border as a savage skirmish ensued that ended with the routing of the Indian force and the capture of their artillery. The war in the Territory was one of small but vicious engagements where Indians were frequently pitted against Indians. Often members of the same tribe held each other in their gunsights in desperate guerrilla actions. They too experienced the true tragedy of the American Civil War.

Brig. Gen. Stand Watie was the only Native American to attain a general's rank in the Civil War. This stubborn Cherokee leader was also the last to surrender his forces on June 23, 1865. (Photo courtesy Civil War Museum, Carthage, Missouri)

Brig. Gen. Stand Watie, the last Confederate general to surrender during the Civil War, originally formed his Cherokee Mounted Rifles at Fort Wayne in 1861. Fort Wayne, near Maysville, Arkansas, was later captured by Federal troops on October 22, 1862. This historical marker along the Arkansas-Oklahoma border in Watts, Oklahoma, marks the original location of Fort Wayne, which was first established in 1839. (Author's collection photo)

Of all the guerrilla bands that roamed the Ozark region during the war, none gained as big a reputation as the group of deadly horsemen who served under William Clarke Quantrill. They were a rough troop of cold-hearted gunmen that included men such as Frank James, Cole Younger, and "Bloody Bill" Anderson, who later formed his own group which included Frank's younger brother, Jesse James. Quantrill was an ex-Kansas schoolteacher who had fought in the pre-war border conflict. Today it is difficult to know what his true nature was. Facts and legends are hard to separate in the case of Capt. William C. Quantrill, who had been awarded his rank for his role in the capture of Independence, Missouri, on August 11. Some considered him a maniacal murderer who craved violence and destruction. Others thought he was a skilled military leader devoted to the Southern cause. Whatever the case, Quantrill was definitely the scourge of Union garrisons posted in towns throughout the Ozark region.

In early November of 1862, Quantrill's 150 partisans were passing through the Ozarks on their way south for the winter. In Benton County they united with a group of 300 Confederate recruits under Col. Warner Lewis. Quantrill and his men occasionally operated with regular troops. The previous August they had served with Col. Jo Shelby in a skirmish with Yankee cavalry along Coon Creek north of Carthage, Missouri. Quantrill and Lewis planned a surprise assault on the Union post at Lamar, Missouri. The garrison consisted of one company of Union Missouri cavalry under the command of Capt. Martin Breeden. The assault was to be made at night with the guerrillas charging in from the north and the regulars entering the town from the south.

At 10:00 P.M. on November 5, Captain Quantrill and his men thundered into Lamar's town square and immediately received a welcoming volley of deadly Union gunfire. Breeden's troops had somehow been forewarned and had taken up positions behind the brick walls of the fortified courthouse. To make matters worse, Lewis and his men did not show up.

Yet the stubborn guerrillas besieged the courthouse for a full hour and a half before their leader finally decided to break off the attack. Setting a third of the town on fire, Quantrill and his men disappeared into the night, leaving six dead in the town square.

Meanwhile, Maj. Gen. Thomas C. Hindman's new Confederate army down in Arkansas had swelled to 11,000 men. Encamped near Van Buren, Arkansas, many of Hindman's troops were reluctant conscripts, drafted against their will to fight for a cause they did not believe in. Yet there were also loyal, determined veterans such as Col. Jo Shelby's Iron Brigade of cavalry. General Hindman decided it was time for his new army to strike the Federals. Fifty miles to the north a Union army of approximately 8,000 troops with 30 artillery pieces was encamped at Cane Hill, Arkansas. A hot skirmish had already taken place there on November 28. Although seriously low on food and ammunition, Hindman nevertheless set forth at dawn on December 3 to do battle with the Yanks.

The Union commander, Brig. Gen. James Blunt, had received greatly exaggerated reports of the size of Hindman's approaching army and wired for reinforcements. Brig. Gen. Francis Herron, encamped more than 100 miles away along Wilson's Creek in Missouri, marched south to Blunt's rescue with 6,000 additional troops and 30 more cannons. Upon receiving news of the approaching enemy reinforcements, Hindman and his officers came up with a daring plan for victory. A feint attack would be made on Blunt at Cane Hill while the main body of troops would outflank him and attack Herron before the two Federal forces could unite. After defeating Herron, the Confederate army would then turn back south and attack Blunt. The plan was elaborate and bold, but totally unsuccessful.

On the night of December 6, Hindman's troops appeared to be encamped near Blunt's army. The Federals could easily see their foes' campfires in the distance. Yet the fires were kept burning by only a small skeleton force of cavalry under

Little remains today of the Arkansas-Indian Territory border community of Cane Hill, Arkansas, which hosted numerous skirmishes during the Civil War.

Thomas C. Hindman, who had led Confederate troops in numerous battles throughout southern Missouri and northern Arkansas, created many enemies as a result of his political radicalism. Fleeing to Mexico after the War for a period, he later returned to his hometown of Helena, Arkansas, where he promised "to abide in good faith by the existing order of things." The legacy of hatred toward him, however, resulted in his being assassinated by an unknown party on September 27, 1886. He is pictured here on October 22, 1865, with his children Susie, Tom, and Biscoe. (Photo courtesy Mrs. Lewis Powell, Phillips County Museum, Helena, Arkansas)

Col. James Monroe while the main body of the army was nearing Herron's position 12 miles away. At dawn on December 7, the Confederate advance guard tore into Herron's cavalry which fled in a wild stampede that was finally stopped around 7:00 A.M. by General Herron himself who personally shot one cowardly Yank from his saddle. By 10:00 A.M. Hindman's entire army was pitted against Herron's force at Prairie Grove, Arkansas. The small community consisted of one church, two or three farm houses, and a couple of hostile armies.

Meanwhile, Colonel Monroe kept up a deceptive series of skirmishes and feint attacks against General Blunt who nevertheless came to realize he had been tricked. Marching north to link up with Herron, he was still unaware of his enemies' location until he heard the distant sounds of embattled artillery. Pressing his troops rapidly toward Prairie Grove, Blunt arrived on the scene at 2:00 P.M. much to the relief of General Herron and his exhausted men. Herron's force had marched 110 miles, much of it through hill country, in only three days, going into battle almost immediately upon their arrival in the area. Their amazing ordeal rivals even the great marches of Stonewall Jackson's famous "Foot Cavalry" in Virginia's Shenandoah Valley. Taking overall command of the combined Union forces, General Blunt continued the battle with renewed fury, throwing fresh troops into the thick of the fight. By this time, Hindman's men were concentrating on the defensive, stubbornly holding their high ridge against the repeated lashes of long Blue lines hurled at them from the Illinois River valley below Prairie Grove.

The terrible fighting continued until darkness fell. The Federals, whose superior artillery had been the major factor in saving them from defeat that day, finally withdrew beyond the range of Rebel guns. The Confederates held the field but another day of battle appeared imminent. General Hindman, with no food for his hungry troops and not enough ammunition for another day of battle, reluctantly chose to

Typical of Confederate infantrymen who fought in the Ozark region during the War are these young veterans of the Battle of Prairie Grove, Arkansas. (Photo courtesy Civil War Museum, Carthage, Missouri)

withdraw toward Van Buren, Once again, a lack of supplies had resulted in a major Southern defeat in the Ozarks. Slipping away in the darkness, the Confederates did not reveal their quiet withdrawal to the Federals who rested on their rifles during the night. One hundred seventy-five Union troops lay dead on the field, 813 had been wounded, and another 252 were missing. A number of the Union dead from General Herron's hard-marching infantry had no wounds upon their bodies; they had died from sheer exhaustion. Confederate battle losses included 164 killed, 817 wounded, and 336 missing. Scattered among a portion of the Southern dead were numerous unspent lead bullets, purposefully discarded from their paper cartridge wrappers. Many of the draftees, sympathetic to the Union, had fired harmless blank rounds at the U.S. troops.

In the chaotic darkness following the battle, General Blunt sent a messenger under a white flag to General Hindman requesting a long truce starting at sunrise the next morning so that he might bury his dead and care for the wounded. Naturally, Hindman readily agreed. When daylight revealed that he had made a truce with a defeated foe, Blunt was furious. However, in the honor-bound tradition of those days, he had no choice but to abide by the agreement, thus allowing the Confederates an extra margin of safety in their retreat.

During Hindman's march back to Van Buren, his army began to steadily dissolve away. Desertion became rampant among his starving, ragged troops. The cavalry had to separate from Hindman's main force, marching 100 miles east of Van Buren where enough forage for their horses could be found. Blunt and Herron, upon receiving fresh supplies, pushed southward, trailing the remnants of the demoralized Southern army. The Federals raided Van Buren and Fort Smith with General Hindman helpless to resist their advance. The Yanks captured many prisoners and destroyed a great deal of Confederate property including several steamboats on the Arkansas River laden with precious supplies for Hindman's destitute troops.

The year 1862 had brought defeat for the Southern Cause in the Ozark region. Although the conflict in the Ozarks would continue, the South had in fact already lost the war in that area.

CHAPTER 3

The Ozarks Burn 1863

Late in December of 1862 a large Confederate cavalry raid into Missouri was ordered for the purpose of taking Federal pressure off the Southern forces in Arkansas. Thus on December 31, Brig. Gen. John S. Marmaduke, a veteran of the Battle of Prairie Grove, marched over 2,000 Missouri cavalrymen north from Lewisburg, Arkansas, and by January 4 they were in Missouri. A graduate of West Point, Marmaduke was a tall, wealthy, young man whose father had been governor of Missouri and whose uncle was none other than Claiborne F. Jackson himself. Marmaduke's first action of the war had been the inglorious skirmish at Boonville in 1861. Yet since that time he had distinguished himself on other fronts including the monumental Battle of Shiloh, Tennessee. Marmaduke's raiding force consisted of Col. Jo Shelby's brigade, Col. Emmett MacDonald's regiment, and Quantrill's guerrillas without Quantrill himself who was on a trip to Richmond, Virginia, seeking a colonel's commission in the Confederate Army. Interestingly enough, Quantrill's men had recently rescued Col. Jo Shelby and his staff from capture along the Fayetteville-Prairie Grove road in northwest Arkansas. A small scouting party which included Frank James, and possibly his younger brother Jesse, were returning to camp when they found Colonel Shelby and his staff completely surrounded by a Federal regiment. Although they were very few in numbers, the party stormed into Shelby's position with such fury the Federals scattered, giving Shelby and his staff time to escape.

The raiders' first objective was a Federal post known to the Confederates as Fort Lawrence. Called Beaver Station by the Yanks, the fort was located on Beaver Creek in Taney County, Missouri. The post protected the Lawrence Mill which was actively grinding meal for the Union army. The fort also served as a base for scouting patrols and was garrisoned by approximately 100 Union militiamen. It consisted of a large two-story blockhouse made of thick logs with musket portholes in its walls. Approximately 10 log cabins near the structure served as barracks for the troops. General Marmaduke dispatched flamboyant Col. Emmett MacDonald with 270 Missouri troopers to destroy the Yankee fort.

Early on the frosty morning of January 6, MacDonald's men stormed the fort and took its garrison by surprise. The fight was over within a few minutes with the post's commander, Maj. William Turner, being wounded and six of his men killed. The Rebels captured a great amount of supplies and foodstuffs as well as 400 muskets which they buried. Colonel MacDonald ordered the fort burned and, before galloping off to rejoin the main force, paroled the captured militiamen. Under the parole agreement, prisoners were sent home after giving their word of honor not to fight again until notification that the other side had received an equal number of parolees.

Meanwhile, General Marmaduke and his main force had been pressing toward Springfield, the primary objective of the raid. This town was the principal supply base for Federal operations in southwest Missouri and northwest Arkansas, but there was yet another town to take before reaching Springfield. In Marmaduke's route of march lay Ozark, Missouri, where a Union post had been established. The Confederates' approach to Ozark was cautious and every man was ready for action, but the Yanks had been warned of their

These unidentified Union cavalrymen of the 7th Kansas Cavalry are typical Federal troops who rode and fought throughout the Ozark region. (Photo courtesy Civil War Museum, Carthage, Missouri)

enemies' impending arrival and had abandoned the village, allowing the Rebs to enter unopposed. The military installation was burned and the march north continued.

At dawn on January 8, General Marmaduke was finally near Springfield, and he paused to await the return of Colonel MacDonald. Marmaduke was also hoping that Col. Joseph C. Porter and his brigade of raiders had received his order to join him. Porter's 825 cavalrymen were also moving north in Missouri, but were to the east of Marmaduke's 2,000 troops and heading toward their own objective, Union installations near Hartville. About 10:00 A.M. MacDonald and his victorious regiment arrived; however, Porter was nowhere in sight. He had not received Marmaduke's orders and would be sorely missed by the young general in the impending battle.

Shortly after MacDonald's arrival, Marmaduke commenced his attack on Springfield. In command of the town's Union garrison was Brig. Gen. Egbert B. Brown, who had only received word of the raiders' approach the day before. Mustering all the extra strength he could gather from local militia groups and citizen volunteers, Brown was determined to hold his ground. Springfield's defenses were slim, but a series of four small forts around the community served as strong points for troop positions. The defenders also had several cannons which they hurriedly deployed for action.

General Marmaduke's men appeared on the edge of the frost-bitten prairie southeast of town, unlimbered their artillery, and commenced firing. The ensuing struggle lasted the rest of the day. As darkness fell, General Brown's makeshift army still retained its hold on most of Springfield while the Confederates held only one captured cannon and the ruins of a few charred buildings. Over 30 Union men lay dead or dying with another 195 wounded including General Brown who was shot off his horse within town by a sniper believed to be a Springfield resident with Southern sympathies. The next morning General Marmaduke, with 70 dead and 200 wounded, decided the town was not worth the cost of further casualties.

Marmaduke rode off to link up with Colonel Porter who had captured the 40-man Federal garrison at Hartville on January 9. The post's fortifications were destroyed by the raiders as were the abandoned facilities at nearby Hazelwood the very next day. Four miles east of Marshfield, General Marmaduke, whose force had captured and burned the abandoned Union facilities at that town as well as the post at nearby Sand Springs, finally found Porter and his men. The two rampaging Rebel forces were united and preparations were made for a swift return to Arkansas.

However, on January 11, a few miles south of Hartville, a sizeable Union force under Col. Samuel Merrill attacked the raiders from the north. After a short skirmish, Merrill withdrew into Hartville and prepared for a major confrontation. Marmaduke obliged him and from 11:00 A.M. to the middle of that winter afternoon the town of Hartville was a blazing battlefield. At last most of Colonel Merrill's force withdrew, having suffered 7 killed, 64 wounded, and 7 missing. The Confederates had 12 killed, 96 wounded, and 3 missing. Among the dead was Col. Emmett MacDonald. Marmaduke, Shelby, and Porter sustained wounds.

The next day General Marmaduke began his long march back to Arkansas. It was a journey of severe hardship for his troops and their horses who endured a bitter winter storm while crossing the frozen Ozark countryside. Although he had failed to take Springfield, Marmaduke's raid had indeed lifted some of the Federal pressure off Confederate forces in Arkansas by diverting the attention of many Union troops northward. In April of 1863, General Marmaduke once again led a raid into Missouri, this time into the southeast corner of the state. His main objective was the Union supply depot at Cape Girardeau, Missouri, which he failed to take because of its strong defenses. Nevertheless, on April 26, Col. Jo Shelby succeeded in driving back Federal forces outside

Quantrill guerilla forces in action. (Reenactment photos)

Union cavalry forming a line in anticipation of enemy contact.
(A reenactment photo)

the town in a delaying action to cover the withdrawal of Marmaduke's main force. Retreating to their fortifications, the Yanks took cover as Shelby opened fire with his artillery. Tense skirmishing also occurred outside the Ozark region at Chalk Bluff on May 1 when Marmaduke's troops crossed the St. Francis River on their way back to Arkansas. Marmaduke's Cape Girardeau raid failed to accomplish much of anything other than misery among his own men who were forced to struggle through the region's mosquito-infested swamps during the fruitless ordeal. Upon his arrival at Confederate headquarters in Jacksonport, Marmaduke reported his losses as 30 killed, 60 wounded, and 120 missing.

Meanwhile, guerrilla warfare intensified. On May 18 a detachment of 40 Federals, most of whom were African-American troops of the 1st Kansas Colored Infantry Regiment, were foraging for corn at a farm near Sherwood, Missouri. Without warning, they were suddenly surprised by Maj. Thomas Livingston and nearly 70 of his Jasper County partisans who burst from the nearby woods with guns blazing. The Yanks were routed with 18 of their number killed. The guerrillas had only two men wounded in the action and captured 5 wagons, 30 mules, and a good supply of guns and ammunition. The next day, vengeful troops from the Union regiment's camp arrived in the area with 300 infantrymen and at least 100 cavalrymen. Livingston's band eluded the force, but the village of Sherwood, a frequent base for the guerrilla forces, was put to the torch. The community was completely destroyed and was never to be rebuilt. Thus Sherwood was added to the growing list of Ozark communities that lay in ruins. By now most of the Ozark region was essentially in a state of anarchy. Destroyed homes and murdered citizens had become commonplace in the region.

Just a few miles from Sherwood lived a settler who had tried to remain neutral during the war. John C. Cox had established a general store and post office near his cabin home and named his tiny family settlement, Blytheville. In June of

1863, Blytheville was raided by Livingston's men and Cox's home was pillaged and burned. What Cox may have done to incur the wrath of Livingston is not known. However, it was extremely difficult for anyone in the Ozarks to remain totally neutral through the war without angering one side or the other at some point. As an example, when a scouting patrol of Yankee cavalry or a hungry band of Rebel guerrillas stopped at a man's home and demanded food, he would have little choice but to give them what they wanted. Yet later, word would get around to the other side that he had given aid to the enemy. His punishment for such acts of treason often meant the destruction of his home and perhaps even his death. Cox may have been killed by the men who burned his home had it not been for the heroism of one of his daughters. Sensing that the raiders were intending to shoot her father, Sally Cox quickly moved in front of John, shielding him with her body. At the sight of this act of bravery, the raiders rode away, physically harming no member of the Cox family. Thus John Cox survived the war to become the founding father of a mining boom town named Joplin which still stands on the site of what was once the charred ruins of Blytheville, Missouri.

On July 11, Major Livingston led approximately 100 of his guerrillas on a raid at Stockton, Missouri. Only 13 Union militiamen were present but they were secure within the courthouse listening to a political speech when the howling band of raiders arrived. In the span of no more than 20 minutes, Livingston and three of his men lay dead outside the building. Three militiamen were killed and two wounded. Fifteen wounded guerrillas were later discovered abandoned near the town they had failed to capture.

The summer of 1863 was a major turning point in the war as strategic Union victories in July sealed the fate of the Confederacy. While the monumental Battle of Gettysburg raged in Pennsylvania and the siege of Vicksburg, Mississippi, drew to a close, gunfire echoed along the banks of Cabin Creek in

Like many citizens of the Ozark region, Cherokees in the bordering Indian Territory were also divided in their loyalties. Zeke Proctor, a Cherokee political leader, joined the Union forces at Fort Gibson. Here, Proctor is pictured in his uniform with two pistols and rattles from rattlesnakes in his hat band. After the war, Proctor became a leader in the movement to preserve Cherokee treaty rights with the United States. Accused of many murders along the Arkansas-Indian Territory border, Proctor was pardoned by President U. S. Grant in order to bring peace to the Indian Territory. (Photo courtesy Elizabeth Walden, Watts, Oklahoma)

Indian Territory. From July 1 to 2 a fierce attempt by Col. Stand Watie to capture a Union supply train of 300 wagons was thwarted by a hard-fighting Union escort. The desperate action at Cabin Creek was a prelude to a much larger battle in the Territory two weeks later about 20 miles southwest of Fort Gibson. On July 17, 3,000 Union troops under Gen. James Blunt surprised nearly 6,000 Indians and Texans under Brig. Gen. Douglas H. Cooper in camp at Honey Springs in what is now eastern Oklahoma.

Cooper was a former U.S. Indian Agent who, despite his fondness for liquor, was highly respected by the Choctaw Tribe, a people whom he honestly served before and after the war. A Mexican War veteran, he had led Confederate forces to victory at the Battle of Newtonia and had fought Blunt before at Fort Wayne in the autumn of 1862. At Honey Springs, Cooper was awaiting the arrival of 3,000 reinforcements from Fort Smith, Arkansas, before proceeding with a plan to advance on the Union stronghold at Fort Gibson. However, Blunt's strike on the Honey Springs camp foiled Confederate military strategy in Indian Territory.

In the center of General Blunt's battle line on July 17 was the 1st Kansas Colored Infantry, a regiment which had been shot to pieces the previous spring near Sherwood, Missouri, and whose troops had helped defend the Union supply wagons at Cabin Creek. At Honey Springs they exchanged a deadly volley of fire with Cooper's battle-hardened Texans who were dangerously close. After a full 20 minutes of blazing action, the Texans gave way, losing one of their battle flags in the bloody clash with the dauntless African-American soldiers. These former slaves had been warned before the battle that the Southerners would take no black prisoners.

James O'Neill, a newspaper artist-correspondent assigned to cover General Blunt's activities, witnessed a dramatic charge by the 6th Kansas Cavalry Regiment upon the Confederate supply depot at Honey Springs. His pen and ink drawing of the cavalry line galloping forward with upraised sabers appeared in the nationally popular tabloid, *Leslie's Illustrated Newspaper*.

The action at Honey Springs lasted only four hours as a steady rain forced the tired Confederates from the field. Despite Cooper's numerical superiority, he had been outgunned. Blunt had 12 artillery pieces in action compared to Cooper's four. Also the ill-equipped Confederate Indians had inferior small arms, while Blunt's infantry carried standard army issue Springfield rifles and his cavalry had up-to-date carbines as well as pistols. Much of the Confederate gunpowder supply had been poorly protected from intermittent rains and had become wet and useless even before the battle began. Cooper listed his casualties as 137 killed and wounded with 47 taken prisoner. Blunt reported his losses as only 17 killed and 60 wounded. Honey Springs, Oklahoma, was the most decisive battle in Indian Territory and firmly established Union dominance of the region.

On September 22, Col. Jo Shelby thundered into his home state of Missouri with his daring cavalrymen on a month-long raid that destroyed over a million dollars worth of Federal supplies. His troops were to fight 10 actions and ride as far north as the Missouri River before the raid was over. This young Southern aristocrat, originally from Kentucky, owned a hemp plantation at Waverly, Missouri, and had first gained his fiery reputation as a bold leader in the pre-war border conflict between Missouri and Kansas.

Passing through the Missouri Ozarks, Shelby reached Neosho where his force encountered nearly 200 Union militiamen on October 4. In preparation for the attack, his men attached sprigs of red sumac bushes to their hats to discern each other from the enemy, for they looked very much like Yanks themselves. According to Maj. John Edwards, Shelby's adjutant, the Confederate government did not issue uniforms or weapons to Shelby's troops, so they utilized whatever they could capture or find, including Union uniforms. This was a very common practice among Southern soldiers in

Confederate Brig. Gen. Joseph Orville (Jo) Shelby proved to be one of the best Confederate cavalry commanders in the Civil War. Frank and Jesse James, who later gained national notoriety as leaders of the James-Younger outlaw gang, were guerilla force leaders who supported Shelby in many battles and skirmishes in the Ozarks. Shelby credited Frank James for helping to save his life during a skirmish along the Fayetteville-Prairie Grove road in northwest Arkansas. (Photo courtesy State Historical Society of Missouri, Columbia)

the half-forgotten Trans-Mississippi theater. Retreating to Neosho's square, the Federals took refuge in the courthouse and Shelby opened fire with his artillery, forcing their surrender. At least five Federals were killed and a number wounded before the militia surrendered. Confederate losses were 7 killed and 22 wounded.

Also on October 4, Shelby's raiders pillaged and burned the town of Bower's Mill which had the reputation of being a command center for Union militia operations in the area. Continuing his march north, Shelby captured the garrison of 50 militiamen at Greenfield and burned its courthouse fort. It was to the Confederates' advantage to leave all brick courthouses in Missouri as charred, gutted-out ruins because Union troops frequently made military strongholds out of the structures. Shelby moved on to Stockton where Maj. Tom Livingston had met his fate over two months earlier. The guerrilla leader had not had the advantage of artillery as Shelby now did and 25 Yanks soon surrendered and their courthouse was burned. The raiders' next objective was Humansville where they skirmished with the town's garrison of 150 troops. A few men were lost before they surrendered.

Pressing north to the Missouri River, Colonel Shelby was finally turned back by the Federals at Marshall on October 13. With overwhelming numbers of enemy troops in close pursuit, he raced back toward Arkansas. Shelby reached Carthage, Missouri, on October 17 and proceeded to set up camp near the town at the Kendrick farm. One battalion of cavalrymen from the Carthage locale received permission from Shelby to occupy the town itself that night. Major Pickler, in command of the detachment, failed to post guards.

At dawn Shelby and his men were aroused by the sounds of artillery and rifle fire from the direction of town. A strong force of Union cavalry under Brig. Gen. Thomas Ewing had surprised the Confederates in Carthage and captured Major Pickler and 30 of his men. Ewing, whose brother-in-law was none other than Gen. William T. Sherman, had recently

The Southern cavalry charging into action on an Ozark battlefield. (A reenactment photo)

become infamous among Southerners for his "Order Number Eleven." While Ewing was district commander along the Missouri-Kansas border, he resolved to cut down civil support for Rebel guerrillas in the region. To accomplish this, he issued Order Number Eleven which forced thousands of Missouri citizens to immediately evacuate nearly all of three counties and part of a fourth.

Colonel Shelby dispatched five companies to hold Ewing in check at Carthage while his main force escaped south. The Yanks were held back for one hour of blazing action in and around the town before the Confederate rear guard swiftly galloped off to rejoin the main force. Shelby eluded his pursuers and successfully continued his swift return to the Confederate lines in Arkansas where he received a promotion to brigadier general. There is no record of the number of casualties in the action of October 18 which is frequently referred to as the Second Battle of Carthage.

In October, Col. William Clarke Quantrill and his guerrillas, now 300 to 400 strong, again passed through the Ozarks. Each fall as the trees shed their leaves, depriving the guerrillas of their protective cover, they would head south for the winter. This time, however, they had an added incentive for reaching the safety of Confederate territory. On August 21, they had gunned down 150 Union citizens in Lawrence, Kansas, and burned the entire town to the ground. Union men in both Kansas and Missouri cried out for revenge.

Quantrill's route of march brought his force to the vicinity of a Federal outpost on the edge of the Ozark region just over the Kansas border in what was then called the Cherokee Neutral Land. The post was known as Fort Blair and was located near Baxter Springs where the first "cow town" in Kansas would thrive immediately after the war. The post had been built to protect and facilitate communications and supplies between Fort Scott, Kansas, and Fort Gibson in Indian Territory. It consisted merely of some log cabins surrounded by an earth embankment about four feet high. Cavalry lieutenant

James B. Pond was in command of the post's garrison of 155 men consisting of one company of a regiment of former slaves, the 2nd Kansas Colored Infantry, and two companies of the 3rd Wisconsin Cavalry.

On the morning of October 6, 60 cavalry troops were sent out from Fort Blair on a foraging expedition. By noon most of the remaining 95 troops had gathered for their lunch which was soon to be interrupted by the rude arrival of some very unexpected company.

Quantrill had learned of Fort Blair's existence earlier that day when he captured a nearby Federal wagon train. Sizing up the situation upon reaching the outskirts of the post, Quantrill split his force in half and ordered one group to attack from the wooded area that bordered three sides of the fort while he took the rest of his men and moved around to the prairie on the post's northern side. Among the bushwhackers' first victims were three men out target shooting with five other soldiers some distance from the fort. One of the casualties was an army scout name Johnny Fry who had gained nationwide notoriety before the war as "Pony Johnny," one of America's first Pony Express riders. The guerrillas got the drop on Johnny and his comrades, never giving them a fair chance to demonstrate their shooting skills.

A sudden burst of gunfire from the woods sent Lieutenant Pond's men scrambling for their weapons. There was little time to react before this charging horde of violent Missouri farm boys were nearly on top of them. Yet Pond rallied his troops and drove the attackers back into the woods and brush. The soldiers of the 2nd Kansas Colored Infantry fought like demons. African-American troops gained a reputation as fierce fighters during the war. Their combat ability was largely gained from sheer desperation in battling a merciless foe. The previous June, Gen. Edmund Kirby Smith, commander of all Confederate forces in the Trans-Mississippi Department, had issued an official order that all black troops and their white officers be given no leniency in battle. They were to be killed rather than taken prisoner.

For half an hour the guerrillas blasted at Fort Blair. However, the Yanks, with the aid of a howitzer manned by Lieutenant Pond himself, held back the deadly partisans. For his heroic efforts in defending Fort Blair and its garrison, James Pond would later receive the Congressional Medal of Honor.

Quantrill was pondering whether or not to resume the attack when he received word of a column of wagons approaching along the road from Fort Scott. It was none other than Gen. James Blunt's personal escort and headquarters train on the way to Fort Smith, Arkansas, and in a buggy with a young lady by his side was General Blunt himself. Blunt was on his way to Fort Smith because trouble was expected there from Confederate forces. This hero of Prairie Grove and Honey Springs had captured Fort Smith a little more than a month before, and he did not intend to lose it. Blunt left Fort Scott on October 4 with an escort of 100 cavalry and a military band. Also with him was his adjutant, Maj. Henry Curtis, son of Gen. Samuel Curtis.

When approximately 400 yards from Fort Blair (Blunt did not know of the earlier fight there), he halted his column to enable his escort and wagons to close up. At this time Quantrill organized his men, who as usual were dressed in various articles of captured Union uniforms, into two lines and positioned them in full view of Blunt and his escort. The general at first thought they were an escort from Fort Blair sent out to greet him! His band was even preparing a musical salute when the approaching horsemen broke into a charge and opened fire. Blunt's entire escort scattered like scared rabbits.

Catching up to their horrified victims, the bushwhackers slew their foes. The only man Quantrill lost in this assault was one who was blown out of his saddle by gunfire from the retreating bandwagon. It was the band's last performance for soon afterward one of the wagon's wheels fell off, hurling the musicians to the ground. Frantically, the terror-stricken men

William Clarke Quantrill, a former Kansas schoolteacher, formed a guerilla band from mostly young Missouri-Kansas border farm boys in support of the Confederate cause. Under his leadership and that of his lieutenants, Bloody Bill Anderson and George Todd, these guerilla forces became the bloodiest and most feared of the Civil War. Quantrill left the Ozarks with a few of his followers shortly after participating in numerous skirmishes in northwest Arkansas. He was killed in a skirmish at Wakefield, Kentucky. (Photo courtesy James Farm Museum)

waved their handkerchiefs as truce flags but were nevertheless slain on the spot. Their limp bodies were thrown into the wagon which was then set on fire. With the band was newspaper artist-correspondent James O'Neill who had witnessed Blunt's victory at Honey Springs in July. O'Neill suffered the same fate as the bandsmen, becoming the only correspondent to be killed in action during the Civil War.

The massacre continued with few escaping. Among the fortunate souls who did survive was General Blunt who mounted a swift horse and jumped a wide ravine ahead of his pursuers. As for the young lady, the wife of an army officer stationed at Fort Smith, she showed no hesitation in dropping feminine manners long enough to straddle a horse and race from the scene. Few were as lucky as Blunt. Out of the 100 men with him that day, over 80 were killed. Among the dead was Major Curtis.

After it was all over, Quantrill merrily boasted, "By God, Shelby could not whip Blunt; neither could Marmaduke, but I whipped him." Indeed he had. Besides killing over 80 percent of Blunt's men, Quantrill had captured ten supply wagons, a fine ambulance, two stands of Union colors, and Blunt's own sword. But perhaps he felt most jubilant over his mistaken belief that Blunt himself was among the dead.

The victorious guerrilla chief decided not to resume his attack on Fort Blair. After a period of drunken celebration, Quantrill and his men saddled up, leaving the troops at the outpost to handle the task of gathering for burial the scores of lifeless bodies scattered across the prairie. The guerrillas' casualty count at Baxter Springs was light. Only two were killed and two wounded in the assault on Fort Blair and one killed and one wounded in the attack upon General Blunt. The casualty count in the fort revealed nine troops killed and ten wounded. It was a bad day for the little post but a worse one for General Blunt who struggled into the fort that night accompanied by a few of his surviving men. His reputation as a bold fighter was severely tarnished. Blunt's noteworthy

*Cole Younger, the ex-guerilla leader and member of the James-Younger outlaw gang. After his release from the Minnesota State Prison, Cole became a very popular personality. He traveled throughout the nation giving lectures on "**What Life Has Taught Me**" and appeared in Wild West shows of the period. He died of natural causes on March 26, 1916.* (Photo author's collection)

military accomplishments would forever be overshadowed by his humiliating defeat at Baxter Springs by a band of hate-filled guerrilla farm boys led by the notorious Col. William C. Quantrill.

After Quantrill's victory at Baxter Springs, the proud guerrilla forces rode south to spend the winter in Texas. Jesse and Frank James, Cole Younger, and other Missouri farm boys who would later become the feared James-Younger gang, followed Quantrill to Texas. During this period they often visited their friend John Shirley who had left Carthage, Missouri, shortly before the town was burned and established a hotel and saloon in Scyene, Texas. There the James brothers and the Youngers got to know Shirley's daughter Myra Maebelle. Myra, who greatly admired these heroic Missouri farm boys, showered them with her affections, especially Cole Younger, whose mother had also moved to Scyene to escape the infamous "Order Number Eleven." Myra Maebelle Shirley was an accomplished pianist and entertained her guerrilla friends at her father's saloon. Although Cole Younger always denied having children, Myra Maebelle, later to become the notorious Belle Starr, fell in love with Cole during this period, and it would later be rumored that Cole was the father of Belle's first child, Rose Pearl.

In 1863, Union forces took the Confederate garrison at Fort Smith, which then became the Union's Western anchor of defense along the Arkansas River. From here, the Union worked to subdue rampant guerilla activity in the region throughout the remainder of the war. (Photos courtesy UALR Archives, Little Rock, Arkansas)

The Fort Smith garrison on the Arkansas River bordering Indian Territory was the main Confederate staging base for campaigns at Cane Hill, Pea Ridge, Prairie Grove, and others in northwest Arkansas, southwest Missouri, and Indian Territory.

CHAPTER 4

The Lost Cause 1864-65

In the spring of 1864, Quantrill's partisans returned from this wild, free-booting time in Texas to begin another season of guerrilla warfare. Passing through the Ozarks, Quantrill threatened a fortified Union camp at Carthage on May 18, then once again raided Lamar, Missouri. He struck at dawn on May 20, 1864. Charging into what was left of the charred town, over 100 rampaging bushwhackers caught the small Union cavalry garrison by surprise. Scattering the Yanks in every direction, it looked as if Quantrill would have revenge for his thwarted 1862 attack on the town. But a sergeant and nine other troopers managed to take cover in the partially ruined brick courthouse where the garrison's rifles were stored. The numerous weapons were each loaded with "buck and ball," which was a popular military gun charge consisting of one large lead ball and several buckshot rammed down the barrel on top of a hefty measure of powder. The 10 desperate defenders began blasting away at the frenzied horsemen outside their walls. Soon the assault began to resemble a daytime version of the November 5, 1862, debacle. After two unsuccessful charges on the courthouse, Quantrill moved on in search of easier prey.

Meanwhile, trouble soon developed across the Arkansas border once again. Confederate general Douglas Cooper advanced against the Union stronghold at Fort Smith just outside the southern edge of the Ozark region. On July 27 a detachment from Cooper's force, consisting of Confederate Indians and Texans led by Col. Richard Gano, sprang a devastating surprise attack on a Union cavalry outpost just south of Fort Smith at Massard Prairie. The camp's commander, Maj. David Mefford of the 6th Kansas Cavalry, rallied his men and directed a desperate fighting retreat toward the fortifications of Fort Smith. Yet it was a futile effort, the cavalry's horses had been stampeded and the dismounted troops were soon surrounded by overwhelming numbers of hard-riding Rebel warriors. Finally, 127 Yanks were captured after 11 had been killed and 20 wounded. Gano's losses included 9 dead and 26 wounded.

On July 30, Cooper advanced on Fort Smith with his entire force. Stand Watie and his men helped drive back Union troops before the fort's defenses. This action was followed by an artillery duel until nightfall when Cooper withdrew, marching back to Indian Territory. The failed assault on Fort Smith was the last major defense effort by Confederate Indians outside their Territory.

Just when it seemed that the Confederate Cause in the Ozark region was at last growing too weak to be a serious threat, a major Southern offensive was launched. Gen. Sterling Price, who had been transferred back to the Trans-Mississippi Department, received an order that he had been anxiously awaiting for two and a half years. Gen. Edmund Kirby Smith, department commander, directed him to take charge of a mounted invasion force and cross the Arkansas border into Missouri. St. Louis was to be the main objective and the gathering of new recruits was to be a primary activity of this massive raid. Price himself had high hopes that the expedition would be more than just a raid, but a full-scale campaign to retake the entire state. It was with this in mind that Missouri's Confederate governor, Thomas C. Reynolds, joined the expedition, hoping to be installed as Missouri's chief executive at Jefferson City. Former Missouri governor

Jackson had died of cancer near Little Rock, Arkansas, on December 6, 1862. Earlier in the war, a Union state legislature and governor had been sworn in following Governor Jackson's retreat south.

After successfully eluding Maj. Gen. Frederick Steele's forces in northeast Arkansas, General Price set forth from the town of Pocahontas, Arkansas, on September 19 with 12,000 troops and 14 artillery pieces. However, "Old Pap's" army was poorly armed and ill equipped. Many of his men didn't even have weapons as the invasion began and some 1,000 had no horses. Price's legion of rough-cut troops, made up of Missourians and Arkansans, was organized into three divisions under Maj. Gen. John Marmaduke, Brig. Gen. Jo Shelby, and Maj. Gen. James Fagan. On the same day it left Pocahontas, the "Army of Missouri," as Price named his force, crossed the state line.

September 19, 1864, was also a significant date for the Southern Cause in Indian Territory. Brig. Gen. Stand Watie's Indian Brigade teamed up with Col. Richard Gano's Texas cavalry to overrun a Federal supply train of more than 250 wagons carrying commissary supplies to Fort Gibson valued at one and a half million dollars. The devastating wagon train attack occurred at Cabin Creek, giving Watie revenge for his defeat along that same Creek in July of 1863. During the action, hundreds of terrified mules broke into a blind stampede and plunged over high bluffs overlooking the creek, taking numerous wagons with them.

Although few battles in the West received recognition compared to Gettysburg, Shiloh, Antietam, or Sherman's march to the sea, thousands died in the numerous smaller battles in the West that were as strategically important as those in the Eastern Theater. Considering the sparse population of the Arkansas-Indian Territory border region, the casualty percentage in the West showed higher.

By 1864 the Indian Nations—including the Creeks, Cherokees, and Seminoles—had become divided. The Indian

Territory had become a major battleground, and the Texas Road was the main route to victory, death, or defeat. Federal troops had penetrated south into the Choctaw country to Boggy Depot, a Butterfield Overland Mail station near Atoka. Most Choctaws supported the Southern cause, and their nation provided a good buffer zone for Confederate Texas.

In 1864 the battles being fought in the Indian Nations were over supplies rather than to gain territory. Confederates desperate for rations and ammunition raided often. Gen. Stand Watie captured a Federally owned steamship, the *J. R. Williams*, which was loaded with supplies for Fort Gibson in June of 1864. This led to his promotion to brigadier general.

The Union forces then formed a supply train at Fort Scott, Kansas, to support Fort Gibson—205 wagons, 4 ambulances, and other supply wagons totalling some 300, left Fort Scott. Maj. Henry Hopkins and his 2nd Kansas Cavalry numbering 260 troops traveled with the supply train as a security force. If the Federal campaign was to succeed in Indian Territory, it was most critical to get the supplies to Fort Gibson.

Reaching the Grand River Hudson Crossing, Major Hopkins ordered his Cherokee Regiment led by Lieutenant Waterhouse to remain there while he took the supply train on south 15 miles to Horse Creek.

While camped at Horse Creek on September 17, Hopkins received a dispatch from Fort Gibson telling him about a major Confederate advance northward and ordering him to take the supply train to Cabin Creek. There, Hopkins found a Union force of some 170 Cherokees in place. Under the command of a Lieutenant Palmer, the Cherokee troops had built a stockade and hospital at Cabin Creek. Shortly after Major Hopkins arrived with his supply train, Lieutenant Whitlow arrived with his 3rd Indian Regiment consisting of 140 men, which resulted in a Federal force at Cabin Creek of some 610 troops.

On September 12, the same day Major Hopkins had left Fort Scott with his supply train, Gen. Richard Gano called on

Gen. Stand Watie at Camp Corser to take his force north to intercept the Federal supply train. Watie's force of 2,000 joined General Gano's 1,200 men at the Canadian River Crossing.

On September 16th the combined forces reached the Verdigris River at Sand Town. General Gano reported, "The clouds looked somber and our V-shaped procession grand as we moved forward in this work of death."

Capt. Edgar Barker led his detachments of the 2nd Kansas Cavalry and the 1st Kansas Colored Infantry consisting of some 125 Federal troops. Found making hay along the river valley, Barker deployed his forces in the ravine. Cabin Creek was pooled every 100 yards with lagoons, and the banks were steep. Confederates then attacked the Federals from five locations. Within half an hour the better prepared Federal forces repulsed three Confederate charges. The Black troops had been warned that the Confederates would give them "no quarter," which encouraged them to fight with a tenacity knowing no equal. The battle lasted some two hours as the Confederate forces' strength finally took advantage of the tired Federal resistance. "The setting sun witnessed our complete success as its last lingering rays rested upon a field of blood. Seventy three Federals, mostly Negroes, lay dead," General Gano later wrote about the encounter. Confederates further reported that they captured 85 Federal troops, their hay-mowing machine, and some 3,000 tons of hay in the affair.

Within 24 hours another battle would begin that would bring the Confederacy its greatest victory in Indian Territory. Taking some 400 men toward Cabin Creek, General Gano located the supply train and an immense herd of grazing mules on the prairie. Major Hopkins and his 25-man scouting party found the advancing Confederate force but could not determine the Confederate strength. In the meantime, General Gano ordered Watie to bring forth the rest of the force which arrived at midnight. The two Confederate generals then decided that, since they had been detected they should attack the Federals immediately. Watie's force formed to the left and Gano formed his line to the right while Howell's battery of six cannons formed the center.

Under a full moon which provided a spotlight on the Union positions, Howell's battery let loose with a cannonade that stampeded the supply train mules. Wagons soon became tangled and many wagons went over the 100-foot bluffs along the creek. The barrage completely immobilized the supply train. As dawn broke the Indian regiments charged forward and by 9:00 A.M. General Gano reported that the field was his. Over one million dollars of Federal supplies were in Confederate possession. The some 2,000 Confederate forces received new clothing and food from the Federal supply train which greatly boosted the morale of the weary and threadbare Confederates.

Although the battle of Cabin Creek was one of the most intense in Indian Territory, only 30 men were killed in the action, mostly Union troops. Seven hundred forty mules were captured, along with 130 wagons. Generals Gano and Watie then proceeded south with their captured Federal supply train. On September 28 the weary Confederate forces arrived at Camp Bragg, two miles south of Johnsons Depot on the south side of the Canadian River. This Confederate force, consisting mostly of dedicated Indian and African-American troops had traveled over 400 miles in 14 days and successfully deterred the Union army's advance into Indian Territory. The battle of Cabin Creek was the last serious battle in Indian Territory although General Stand Watie and his "Waties Rifles" would never let the Federals rest until the war's end.

Meanwhile General Price, heading north toward St. Louis, received word at Fredericktown of Federal positions. Spies told him that 8,000 troops were encamped near St. Louis and ready to defend the city. He was also told that a garrison of 1,500 Federals was at the nearby town of Pilot Knob. The old general saw the chance of an easy victory and on September

Maj. Gen. Sterling Price, commander of Missouri Confederate troops and hero of the state's Southern sympathies throughout the War. (Photo courtesy Civil War Museum, Carthage, Missouri)

26, he sent General Shelby northward to destroy the tracks and bridges of the Iron Mountain Railroad, cutting off the Union force at Pilot Knob from St. Louis reinforcements. The rest of Price's army marched toward Pilot Knob until late in the afternoon when they collided with Federals at a spot called Shut-In Gap near the town of Arcadia where indecisive skirmishing took place until darkness fell. At sunrise the struggle resumed with the Federals fighting a delaying action through Ironton to Pilot Knob where their commander, Brig. Gen. Thomas Ewing, ordered his men to take up positions at Fort Davidson. Surrounded by a dry moat ten feet wide and over six feet deep, the fort was an eight-sided structure with a nine-foot high dirt parapet topped with sandbags. An impressive network of trenches beyond its walls provided the fort with outer defenses. Gen. Ewing's force was not 1,500 strong as reported to Price, but actually consisted of no more than 900 men, some of whom were civilian volunteers from the vicinity. However, with four huge siege guns, three howitzers, three mortars, and six field artillery pieces, Ewing's men prepared to hold the fort against the thousands of Confederates massing before them.

That afternoon, after a short and pitifully ineffective bombardment of the fort by four cannons situated on high ground, Price ordered an assault. The high-pitched Rebel yell echoed through the valley as thousands of men hurled themselves into a hideous storm of shot and shell. Three times they charged the walls; three times they failed to take them. The hellish gunfire mowed down scores of brave, young soldiers. A few reached the moat, only to be slaughtered by rifle fire and crude grenades. As the thunder of the guns finally subsided, thick clouds of sulfureous gunsmoke drifted away to reveal a ghastly scene of carnage. The fields before Fort Davidson were covered with nearly 1,000 dead and wounded men. The surviving Confederates bivouacked for the night and prepared to renew the bloody contest in the morning, building ladders to scale the fort's walls. Word that

Fort Curtis, an earthwork position reenforced with sandbags, a key Union position, is typical of Federal artillery positions throughout the Ozarks. This Union position contained nine 32-pound siege guns mounted on rotating platforms. (Photo courtesy Arkansas History Commission, Little Rock, Arkansas)

Three times Confederates charged the walls of Fort Davidson at Pilot Knob, Missouri, and three times they failed to take them. (A reenactment photo)

the hated General Ewing was in command of the Union force no doubt strengthened the resolve of the Southerners.

Inside the fort, Ewing tallied up his casualties, only 75, and made plans to attempt an evacuation that night. Incredibly, he succeeded! At 3:00 A.M. his troops quietly slipped out of the fort, and in the nighttime chaos of battle preparations, the Union force was mistaken by Rebel pickets for friendly troops moving to a new position. An hour after the Yanks abandoned the fort, a slow burning fuse in the powder magazine accomplished its mission, setting off an incredible explosion that shook the surrounding hills and left a huge smoldering crater in the middle of the fort. Not taking a hint, the Confederates believed an accident had occurred within the stronghold and that the survivors would surrender at dawn.

In the morning, Price learned that the fort was his but that Ewing and his men were gone. A subsequent attempt by a portion of the Confederate force to overtake the Federals was unsuccessful. There was no victory for the Confederates to celebrate at Pilot Knob and large numbers of troops began deserting the Army of Missouri soon after the bloody debacle.

Leaving Pilot Knob on September 29, Price marched north. His delay at Pilot Knob had allowed the Federals enough time to rush reinforcements to St. Louis. Deciding against an assault of the heavily defended city, Price sent a small force of Shelby's cavalry to fake an attack there while he marched off with his main force westward to Jefferson City. Upon reaching the outskirts of the state capital on October 7, Price spent the day probing its strong Federal defenses. The following morning he marched off and Thomas C. Reynolds remained a governor without a capital. As the Army of Missouri approached the area of Kansas City, it encountered strong Federal resistance. Finally on October 23, the weary Confederates, now numbering only 9,000, were soundly defeated at Westport by 20,000 Union troops commanded by

Hundreds were left wounded or dead throughout the battlefield as the Confederate battle line moved forward. (A reenactment photo)

Maj. Gen. Samuel Curtis of Pea Ridge fame and Maj. Gen. Alfred Pleasonton, noted cavalry commander from the Eastern Theater. This defeat was followed by a hasty retreat south with the Union army in close pursuit.

Crossing the border into Kansas, Price's desperate army ravaged the land in its path. West of the Ozarks, a portion of the Confederate army, under Generals Marmaduke and Fagan, made a stand at Mine Creek north of Fort Scott, Kansas. The Southerners were routed and hundreds were captured, including General Marmaduke himself.

Crushed and demoralized, most of Price's ragged force nevertheless remained intact and once again entered the Ozark region. Crossing back into Missouri, the Confederates arrived at the charred ruins of Carthage on October 26 and camped for the night. The entire town had been burned by guerrillas on September 22. By October 28 the Confederate army was four miles south of Newtonia and Price decided to set up camp and rest his men and horses for a few days. Yet the relentless Yanks were still in pursuit and the tired and hungry Rebels had just begun to gather corn from a nearby field when the alarm was sounded that the enemy was within sight. Price ordered Shelby to hold them back while the main force continued its retreat. The familiar sounds of battle once again filled the air near Newtonia. When Shelby opened fire on the Federals he met with immediate success and drew close to overrunning them, pushing the Union troops back a mile and a half. It was not the Curtis full force that had surprised the Confederates but merely 1,000 cavalrymen led by Gen. James Blunt. Since his humiliating defeat at Baxter Springs, Blunt had been struggling to regain his military reputation and when he located Price's camp he did not wait for the rest of Curtis' forces to arrive before attacking.

Outnumbered by his foe, Blunt was forced to stretch his battle lines thin. Shelby sensed his opponent's weakness and grouped several units for a mass charge. He sent them roaring into the center of the Union line in a furious headlong

James Butler Hickok, who later became famous as a gunfighter, town tamer, and Old West personality, known as Wild Bill Hickok, acted as a Union spy during the Civil War in the Ozarks. While serving near Yellville, Arkansas, during the War, he had a conflict with the Tutt family. This later resulted in Hickok's infamous gunfight with Tutt in Springfield, Missouri, and Ned Buntline's choosing to feature Hickok in his Western novels. (Photo author's collection)

assault. But with the help of the blazing mountain howitzers of the 1st Colorado Battery, the stubborn Union force repelled the savage onslaught. It is said that during the confusion of the battle, two Union scouts serving as spies slipped from the Confederate lines and galloped away under a hail of bullets. One was shot from his saddle while the other, James B. Hickok, escaped without a scratch. This young scout later gained fame as a fearless Western gunfighter known as "Wild Bill Hickok."

Blunt's men began running low on cartridges as the battle continued. One company of the 3rd Wisconsin Cavalry exhausted its supply of ammunition but still held its position, apparently planning to use their empty carbines as clubs if necessary. Just before Blunt's men suffered the consequences of their leader's impetuous aggression, Brig. Gen. John Sanborn's brigade, accompanied by General Curtis himself, dramatically arrived on the scene to rescue them. Shelby then withdrew and the fast approaching nightfall discouraged any attempt of Federal pursuit.

Continuing its retreat south through early sleet and snow, the Army of Missouri steadily dissolved, losing men to desertion and disease every step of the way. On November 1, the army entered the village of Cane Hill, Arkansas, and licked its wounds for three days. During this time, word arrived in camp that a Southern force was besieging the Union garrison at Fayetteville, 30 miles away. Incredibly, Gen. Fagan sought and gained permission from Price to take 500 men and an artillery battery to participate in the action. On November 2, Fagan ordered his men forward through drifting snow in an assault on the town. However, his demoralized troops refused to advance within range of the Federal rifles. The Yanks retained their hold on Fayetteville and the Civil War in the Ozark region was over. The Army of Missouri trudged off into Indian Territory on a hideous trek to Texas in which freezing weather and disease took a heavy toll on the desperate survivors of this last great raid.

Pro-Union sentiment was high in politically divided northwest Arkansas. The state's only Union artillery unit was raised in Fayetteville, Arkansas, on August 31, 1863. Since such units were familiar with the geography and people of the region, they were most effective against the guerrillas who infested the north Arkansas Ozarks. Some 8,289 Arkansans enlisted in the Federal Army, the majority of whom served in cavalry units. Approximately 1,700 Arkansas Union soldiers died in action. Twenty-five members of this first and only Union Light Artillery Battery from Arkansas had lost their lives when the battery mustered out on August 10, 1864. (Photo courtesy Washington County Historic Society, Fayetteville, Arkansas)

In the wake of the passing armies came another threat. In addition to the ever-present bushwhackers, numerous bands of renegade soldiers, stragglers, and outlaws taking advantage of the war-torn Ozarks roamed the region.

The civilian population of the Ozarks were terrorized by lawless marauders who took whatever they wanted and lived off the land. Peaceful settlers such as Moses and Susan Carver, whose farm was located southwest of Carthage near Diamond Grove, suddenly found themselves at the mercy of ruthless scavengers. Moses was hung by his thumbs from a tree near his cabin as his tormentors attempted to force him to reveal the location of his life's savings. The Carvers' female slave, Mary, and her infant son were kidnapped. The Carvers attempted to locate the two, who were like part of the family rather than slaves. Mary was never found but the child was finally recovered and grew to become the renowned scientist, educator, and humanitarian, George Washington Carver.

With the arrival of spring in the year 1865, many guerrilla bands appeared at their old haunts once again but found conditions had changed. The two major Southern armies east of the Mississippi River surrendered in April. Finally on May 26, the military forces of the Confederate Trans-Mississippi Department were formally surrendered on paper in New Orleans by Gen. E. Kirby Smith's chief of staff, Lt. Gen. Simon Buckner. That spring and summer, scores of Missouri guerrillas grudgingly rode to designated points of surrender. A few chose to go down fighting; but most, tired and longing for peace, accepted reality. The terms of surrender were generous for most. Simply give up your arms and pledge loyalty to the Union, was the only requirement. The Yanks were allowing the "outlaws" to surrender just as if they were regular troops. The guns fell silent as hundreds of battle-weary bushwhackers rode in from the brush. Tired and both physically and emotionally distraught over their years of fighting for a lost cause, most accepted their defeat and returned to their homes to begin their lives again.

The war's last formal surrender of any sizeable force of Confederate troops took place in Indian Territory on June 23, 1865, when Brig. Gen. Stand Watie rode into the capital of the Choctaw Nation and surrendered his hard-riding Rebel warriors. Yet there were those who would not surrender. Gen. Jo Shelby marched his men to Mexico rather than concede defeat. Accompanying Shelby's brigade were other die-hard officers including Gen. Sterling Price and Gen. Thomas Hindman. In Mexico these die-hard Confederates hoped to regroup and make plans for the South to rise again.

It was an uneasy peace that finally came to the Ozarks in the summer of 1865. Old wounds were often slow to heal in the region as bitter grudges and feuds were passed on from one generation to the next. Even much of the brutal vigilante activity of the famous Ozark "Baldknobbers" in the 1880s had wartime roots, as did the actions of numerous outlaw gangs such as the James-Younger gang and others.

Although it is difficult today to imagine these beautiful Ozark hills once echoing with sounds of a bloody conflict, memories of this dramatic period in the region's history continue to influence society of the region. The bravery, self-sacrifice, family divisions, and hardships will always remain as a treasured part of Ozark history.

CHAPTER 5

Lost Treasures of the Civil War

Known for their unique ability to tell stories or to spin a yarn, most any Ozark native whose family has been in the region for several generations can easily recount hundreds of Ozark tales. Stories of outlaws, ghosts, monsters, natural phenomena, Indian love affairs, Spanish treasure, and Civil War incidents are kept alive. This unique part of Ozark culture greatly contributes to the appeal of the region.

Among the most popular of Ozark yarns are tales of Civil War treasure. Certainly the many battles and skirmishes the war brought to the region left an abundance of artifacts such as minié balls, rifles, cannon balls, sabers, bayonets, and other hardware scattered around the numerous battle sites. Today's popularity of historic artifacts has greatly increased the value of such items on the Civil War collectable market. Their finding brings back the reality of a war some of us today have a hard time understanding. Many of the Civil War-era folktales naturally have been altered or exaggerated as they have been passed down from one generation to the next over the years since the great conflict came to an end in 1865. A few such tales of Civil War treasure are as follows.

A payroll officer and two guards were approaching Prairie Grove, Arkansas, with a payroll consisting of gold coins. As they were some one mile away they heard sounds of the raging battle there. Fearing that the payroll might be lost or taken in battle, the party turned and rode to a mountain which is known today as Pinnacle Mountain, along the Hogeye road south of Prairie Grove. There the men buried the payroll and joined their regiment on the battlefield. All three men were mortally wounded in the battle. As the last man lay dying, he told an officer about burying the funds and where the payroll could be found. A few days after the important Prairie Grove conflict, the officer searched the mountain for the money but it was never found. Over the years hundreds have combed Pinnacle Mountain but the elusive gold still remains lost.

Some 20,000 Confederate soldiers wintered in a valley known as Cross Hollows southeast of Rogers, Arkansas. Barracks extended for a mile down the valley. The encampment also served as a supply depot to support the Confederates' advance into Missouri. Realizing the Federal army was approaching rapidly from the north and fearing they might overpower the camp, the commanding officer ordered a retreat. There were not sufficient wagons to carry the stores of rifles, ammunition, and field cannons. A large trench was dug into the south ridge along the valley and the supplies were buried to prevent them from falling into the hands of the Federal army. The Confederate army never returned to Cross Hollows and the extensive cache of Civil War weaponry remains hidden somewhere in this beautiful valley near Beaver Lake in northwest Arkansas.

Callihan Mountain lies along the east side of U.S. 71 in northwest Arkansas. The Patton family whose ancestors acquired a farm on Callihan Mountain shortly after the Civil War still tells the story their ancestor passed along to succeeding generations. A party of Confederates were being pursued by a Federal regiment. Realizing that the Federals were gaining on them and that they soon would all be engaged in battle, the Confederates rode to the top of the mountain where they all placed their money, jewelry, and personal effects into a large tin box and buried the container. A huge stone which took 20 men to move was then rolled over their personal effects. An agreement had been made that those in the party who might survive the impending conflict would later dig up the tin box and distribute its contents to the men's families. All of these soldiers eventually would die on the Pea Ridge battlefield. As one of the Rebels lay dying, he told Private Patton where the box could be found and asked him to see that their families got its contents. At war's end, Patton, remembering the story and the obligation he made to the dying soldier, returned to Callihan Mountain and acquired a nearby farm. There he spent a lifetime searching around the mountain for the stone near a large spring where the cache was buried, but it was never found. Callihan Mountain has since become an exclusive housing addition in northwest Arkansas and the Confederate treasure may now be deeply buried beneath any number of homes or streets on the mountain.

Stories of wagonloads of rifles and cannons being shoved off of river bluffs to prevent capture by advancing Federal troops exist at Edens Bluff on Beaver Lake in northwest Arkansas, at the Big Cabin Creek battle site in eastern Oklahoma, and at many other locations.

Hundreds of other similar tales of buried weaponry or payroll funds exist throughout the Ozarks. Unquestionably, Ozark farm families always hid their money and personal treasures in fruit jars, behind certain chimney stones, or buried under stones or certain fence posts as the war engulfed the land. Banks were not trusted to be a safe location for their savings during the conflict or for many years thereafter. A great many such Ozark farm families were killed by the pillaging bushwhacker parties that roamed the hills or were forced to leave their homes and never return. It is therefore reasonable to assume that hundreds of thousands of dollars may still remain stored away in fruit jars or metal boxes beneath the Ozark landscape.

Those who have seriously researched these stories of Civil War treasure can often be seen exploring old homesteads and sites of Civil War camps, battles, and skirmishes throughout the Ozark regions of southern Missouri, northwest Arkansas, and eastern Oklahoma. A great amount of Civil War history no doubt still lies below the rocky Ozark soil.

CHAPTER 6

Jesse James and the Civil War

The post-war environment which created a great many hardships and discriminating treatment of those who had served in Quantrill's ranks during the war made it most difficult for such ex-guerrillas to return to society. Such men were no longer allowed to vote, hold any political office, or borrow money from any Federal institution. They were even banned from serving in a leadership position within their church. It is therefore of little wonder that many of these desperate and hate-filled men turned into outlaws who directed their criminal activities toward the despised banks and railroads which were mostly owned by Northern interests. Their farms and former lifestyles destroyed, it was extremely difficult for them to overcome the bitterness that had been bred into them for long years. Some also may have felt that the South would eventually rise again. Many of their rights rescinded, they also must have felt that the North owed them a great deal for what had been taken from them both materially and emotionally by the conflict. Although there were numerous outlaw gangs created during this period of reconstruction, Jesse James, his brother Frank, and their former war associates, the Youngers, gained the most notoriety.

John Newman Edwards, after whom Jesse James was to name his son, perhaps was the one most responsible for first creating the notoriety the James-Younger gang obtained. As the editor of the *Kansas City Times*, Edwards, also an ex-Confederate, wrote regular editorials glamorizing the daring exploits of the James-Younger band of outlaws.

Jesse and Frank James were sons of the Rev. Robert Sallee James and Zerelda Elizabeth Cole. Robert, born in Kentucky on July 17, 1818, graduated from Georgetown College in 1843 and continued his graduate studies there until 1848. Becoming a Baptist minister, he met Zerelda at a revival in Stamping Ground, Kentucky. Zerelda was born in Midway, Kentucky, on January 29, 1825. She was the daughter of Richard and Sallie Lindsey Cole. Richard Cole was accidentally killed in a horse accident at an early age. Sallie then married Robert Thomason and they moved to Clay County, Missouri. Zerelda remained in Kentucky under the guardianship of her uncle, James Lindsey, while she finished school at St. Catherine's Academy in Georgetown. The Rev. Robert James and Zerelda were married on December 28, 1841, in her uncle's home in Stamping Ground. While pregnant with her first child, Zerelda joined her mother and stepfather, the Thomasons, in Missouri while Robert remained in Kentucky to finish his graduate studies. Alexander Franklin James was born in Missouri on January 10, 1843.

Joining his wife and son in Missouri in 1845, Robert James acquired a 147-acre farm and log home east of Centerville, now Kearney, Missouri. A second son, Robert, who lived only a few weeks, was born to them on July 19, 1845. Their next child, Jesse Woodson James, was born September 5, 1847, and Susan Lavenia on November 25, 1849.

Thousands rushed to get rich in the California gold fields in the now-famous rush of 1849. Robert James, who had founded three Baptist congregations in Clay County and helped organize the William Jewell College in Liberty, Missouri, joined a wagon train west from Clay County in 1850. He had hoped to establish a gold mining operation in California with his brother Drury James and obtain sufficient wealth to carry out his Baptist missionary work. Leaving

Zerelda and her three small children alone with the family's two slaves he had brought from Kentucky, Robert had hoped to return within a year. Robert's plans and dreams of finding wealth did not materialize, however, as he became tragically ill from food poisoning a short time after his arrival and died in a Placerville, California, gold camp on August 18, 1850.

Two years later, Zerelda married a neighboring farmer, Benjamin Simms, on September 30, 1852. This was not a successful union and although divorce was imminent, Simms conveniently died in a horse accident before their divorce proceedings. Zerelda then met Dr. Reuben Samuel, a graduate of the Ohio Medical College, who was practicing medicine in a store building owned by William James, a brother to Robert, in Greenville, Missouri. Dr. Samuel, who was to become the only father the James children ever knew, and Zerelda were married on September 25, 1855. The Samuels then also had children of their own—Sarah in 1858, John in 1861, Fannie Quantrill in 1863, and Archie Peyton in 1866.

Shortly after Dr. Samuel and Zerelda were married, Kansas abolitionists under the leadership of such religious fanatics as Jim Lane, John Brown, and others began raiding farms along the Missouri-Kansas border country, stealing slaves and taking them to Kansas to be given their freedom. Often barns, homes, and crops were burned by such raiding parties who excused their treachery as "doing the Lord's work." It was under such a reign of terror the James children grew up. What was to become the great Civil War, therefore, began along this Missouri-Kansas border country long before the shot was fired at Fort Sumter in 1861.

As the War Between the States began, most of the residents of Clay County were old Southern families and slaveowners who naturally supported the Confederate cause. Frank James was age 18 when he enlisted in the Confederate Army at Centerville, Missouri, on May 4, 1861.

Shortly after participating in the important battle of Wilson's Creek in Missouri, Frank James became ill with measles

Franklin Alexander James, Jesse James' older brother, joined the Confederate Army and fought in the Battle of Wilson's Creek. Captured there by Federal forces on February 12, 1862, he was forced to pledge allegiance to the Union and was released. He then joined Quantrill's guerilla forces. Following Quantrill to Richmond, Virginia, he was with the guerilla leader when Quantrill was mortally wounded in a skirmish at Wakefield, Kentucky. At the close of the war, Frank surrendered at Samuel's Depot, Kentucky, on July 26, 1865, and returned to Missouri where he joined his brother Jesse, the Youngers, and other former guerilla associates in forming the James-Younger outlaw gang. Five months after his brother Jesse was killed, Frank James surrendered to then Missouri governor Thomas Crittenden in October 1882. Tried and acquitted each time for past crimes of the James-Younger gang, Frank became a model citizen and died of natural causes on February 15, 1915. (Photo courtesy of James Farm Museum)

and was hospitalized in Springfield. The hospital was captured by Union forces. Forced to pledge allegiance to the Union, on April 26, 1862, Frank was released and returned home. Shortly thereafter, Frank left home to join a group of young Missouri farm boys known as Quantrill's guerrilla forces, under the leadership of an ex-Kansas schoolteacher, William Clarke Quantrill. Not officially affiliated with either the Union or Confederate armies, these hate-filled border ruffians became the bloodiest force in the Civil War and greatly contributed to the Confederate efforts throughout Missouri, Arkansas, Kansas, and Indian Territory (now Oklahoma).

Jesse James was only 14 when the war began and was too young to be accepted by the Confederate Army or by Quantrill's irregular forces. While plowing in a field behind his home in late May of 1863, young Jesse was suddenly surrounded by a mounted detail of Union soldiers. Because he refused to answer after being repeatedly asked about the location of his brother Frank and Quantrill's camp, the detail severely whipped Jesse with bull whips and left him bleeding in the field. Half crawling to the house, he found his stepfather Reuben hanging from a tree and his mother desperately trying to cut him down while his young sister Susan and Sarah Samuel watched in horror. Dr. Samuel had been left hanging by the Federal party after several unsuccessful attempts to get information from him about his stepson's whereabouts. He did not die from the hanging but oxygen had been deprived from his brain so long he would remain mentally incapacitated the rest of his life. Although Jesse was now only 15 years of age, the tragic events of the day inspired him to wait no longer and he left to join Quantrill's ranks. Legend tells that Quantrill was reluctant to accept Jesse as a result of his youth, but finally consented with Frank James' assurance that he would be responsible for him. His horsemanship, masterful skill in handling weapons, fearlessness in battle, and natural leadership soon earned Jesse James a

Dr. Rueben Samuel, stepfather to Frank and Jesse James, and their sister Susan, was a loyal supporter of Quantrill's guerilla forces and the cause for which they fought. Seeking information about his stepson Frank and Quantrill's guerilla camps, a Union party hung Dr. Samuel seven times from a tree near his Clay County farm home in late May of 1863. Since he refused to answer, they left Dr. Samuel hanging and moved to the field behind his home where Jesse James was plowing in the fields. The party severely whipped young Jesse and rode away with no answers to their questions. Dr. Samuel did not die from the hanging, but oxygen being deprived from his brain caused him to be mentally incapacitated the rest of his life. These Union actions against their family no doubt contributed to the strong hatred the James brothers developed toward the Union and encouraged them to continue their pillage of Union interests as the James-Younger gang long after the Civil War. (Photo courtesy the Samuel Family)

Jesse Woodson James gained international notoriety after the Civil War as the leader of the James-Younger outlaw gang. Eluding capture for nearly 17 years, Jesse was finally brought down by a reward-seeking associate on April 3, 1882. Too young to join the Confederate Army in 1861, he later joined Quantrill's guerilla forces and served under Capt. Bloody Bill Anderson. Although younger than most of his Missouri-Kansas farm boy associates, he became a leader within the guerilla forces at an early age. Pictured here in a photo made in Platte City, Missouri, in July of 1864, he is wearing a typical guerilla uniform and carrying three pistols. (Photo courtesy James Farm Museum)

great deal of respect throughout the irregular forces. Such respect was first gained in a small but meaningful battle near the village of Centralia, Missouri, on September 20, 1864.

The same day hundreds of Confederate soldiers fell before the guns of Fort Davidson, scores of Union troops also met a cruel fate at Centralia. General Price had sent word to the guerrilla bands of his planned invasion and urged them to support him.

Quantrill's band had splintered into several groups by this time, each being led by the fiercest of his followers. Capt. Bloody Bill Anderson's command included the James brothers and a psychopathic killer, "Little Archie" Clement, who would become Jesse James' close friend. Camping near Centralia on the night of September 26 on the Singleton farm with Anderson and George Todd, another Quantrill officer, some 200 hardened farm boys sat around their campfires discussing Price's invasion and the glorious role they might play in it.

At dawn Bloody Bill took 30 men into town to see what they could learn about Price's advance in the newspapers. Before noon the ruffians had looted numerous stores, robbed an in-coming stagecoach, gotten drunk, and burned the railroad depot. Hearing a train whistle, Anderson's men piled railroad ties across the track. As the engine steamed to a slow stop the guerrillas forced all of the passengers off the train. Some 25 unarmed Union soldiers were on board. After the civilian passengers were robbed and released, the treacherous Anderson ordered the luckless Union men who were on furlough to be "mustered out." Anderson directed his men to gun down the defenseless Yanks. Leaving them in a bloody pile, Anderson's men then burned the train and jubilantly rode back to their camp on Singleton's farm. This, one of the most heartless and bloody events of the Civil War, is a good example of why Anderson had earned the title "Bloody Bill."

Later that day, Maj. A. V. Johnson rode into Centralia with over 150 Union troops, a detachment of the 39th Missouri

Capt. Bloody Bill Anderson, the most feared leader within Quantrill's guerilla forces. Jesse James and others who were to later ride with the James-Younger outlaw gang served under Bloody Bill. (Painting from photograph by Ron Raymer)

Jesse and Frank James, the Youngers, and other hate-filled Ozark farm boys rode with irregular guerilla forces under the leadership of William Clarke Quantrill and his lieutenants, Bloody Bill Anderson and George Todd. Such guerilla forces were not officially attached to any Confederate forces and rode at will in support of the Southern cause. (A reenactment photo)

Infantry. All were mounted and armed only with muzzle-loading rifles. Seeing the results of Anderson's visit to town and learning that he had only 30 men with him, Johnson was determined to hunt Anderson down.

Leaving a portion of his command in town to restore order, Johnson ignored warnings that there were numerous other guerrilla forces in the vicinity and led his column of inexperienced and poorly armed riflemen toward Singleton's farm. As the Union force topped a hill they were shocked to see a deadly force of bushwhackers numbering at least 200 in a battle line ready for action. Johnson then ordered his men to dismount and form a double rank firing line to begin one of the most devastating guerrilla actions of the war.

Anderson led the charge up the hill with some 200 horsemen. The Union rifles responded in a volley of bullets that were for the most part ineffective due to the difficulty of firing down hill. Only three of Anderson's men were lost in the charge. One of these men, named Shepherd, was riding next to Frank James when his head was blown apart by a bullet from the Union's volley. Brains and blood covered Frank's leg. Frenzied horsemen charging the Bluecoats killed and scattered most of the Union force. The courageous Major Johnson stood alone firing his pistol until he was shot down by a young farm boy named Jesse James.

Anderson's men then thundered back to Centralia to wipe out what few men remained from Johnson's command. Only a handful escaped, one of whom was Capt. Adam Theis, the commander of the troops in town. None other than Frank James and Archie Clement pursued the fleeing Union leader.

Anderson's force, along with help from Todd's command, killed some 120 Union men on that bloody day. Bloody Bill would lose his life less than a month later in a carefully planned Union ambush near Richmond, Missouri.

As the guerrilla forces were gradually forced to retreat south, Frank James, Jesse James, Cole Younger, and several other of their friends rode south to Arkansas to assist the already famous Shelby Cavalry Brigade. Jesse James had his first glimpse of Jo Shelby when the party of irregulars rode into his camp along Richland Creek in northwest Arkansas. Following Shelby's command as they rode through the area encountering skirmishes with numerous Federal forces, Frank and Jesse James left the main force in pursuit of a Union detachment along the Fayetteville-Prairie Grove road. Returning, they were surprised to find Shelby and his entire command staff surrounded by a Union force and being asked to surrender. Although the James brothers had only a few men in their party, they stormed into the Union force surrounding Shelby with such surprise and ferocity the Union soldiers scattered allowing Shelby and his staff to escape. Shelby thereafter often praised the bravery of Jesse and Frank James in saving him from capture or death that day.

Quantrill decided to take his men to Kentucky where he felt his guerrilla tactics could be more effective against the Federal onslaught there. Frank James decided to follow Quantrill to Kentucky while Jesse preferred to go with his friends Cole Younger, Jim Reed, and others into Indian Territory and Texas. Jesse participated in a major skirmish around the Arkansas border city of Cane Hill and a story is told there that demonstrates the somewhat arrogant personality young Jesse James had developed over his several months of bloody guerrilla skirmishes throughout the Ozarks. Chasing down a Union soldier on horseback he yelled out to the trooper as he rode alongside of him, "You are about to be sent to join your friends in Hell by Jesse Woodson James." He then shot the soldier from his horse and left him lying in a field.

Jesse and other remnants of guerrilla bands rode into Indian Territory where they participated in the battles at Cabin Creek and other localities before drifting into Texas. Cole Younger's mother had left Lee's Summit, Missouri, to escape the ravages of war and settled in Scyene, Texas, which was only a few miles east of Dallas. John Shirley, who had known and supported the guerrilla bands when they were being formed in his Shirley House Tavern in Carthage, Missouri, also had moved to Scyene. His daughter, Myra Maebelle, had also served the guerrilla forces by carrying important information about Union movements to the guerrilla camps. Shortly before the city of Carthage was burned, John Shirley had left Missouri for Texas and once more established a boarding house and tavern there. John Shirley and especially his vivacious daughter Myra Maebelle, who was destined to later become the notorious Belle Starr, therefore welcomed Jesse James, Cole Younger, and their other associates.

It was during this period that Myra Maebelle Shirley first fell in love with the tall and handsome Cole Younger. Although she would later marry another one of their associates, Jim Reed, in 1866, rumor still exists that Belle's first child, Rose Pearl Reed, born in 1868, was actually the daughter of Cole Younger. Cole always denied ever having any children; however, Pearl Reed strongly resembled Cole and she was known to sometimes use the name of Pearl Younger.

As the war came to an end with Robert E. Lee's surrender at Appomattox Court House, Virginia, on April 9, 1865, the tired guerrilla bands were anxious to return home, surrender, and hopefully renew their former lives as peaceful Missouri farmers.

Frank James, who had been with Quantrill when he was cornered and killed in a barn in Wakefield, Kentucky, rode to Samuel's Depot, surrendered by pledging once again his allegiance to the Union, and soon returned to Missouri.

Jesse James rode to Missouri with a sizeable group of his associates and while carrying a white flag approached the Federal garrison at Lexington, Missouri, with plans to surrender. Suddenly the party was fired upon by the Federals and Jesse was seriously wounded with a bullet in his right lung and in one leg. This unexpected and devastating injury caused Jesse James major pain for the rest of his life. Also this unprovoked attack by Union forces while he was attempting to surrender no doubt greatly affected Jesse James and contributed to his choosing to follow the outlaw trail for the rest of his short and violent life. Jesse James was never again known to officially surrender.

The James brothers, the Youngers, and many of their associates had extreme difficulties in trying to adjust to a society that had prevented them from being normal citizens as a result of deprivations placed on ex-members of guerrilla forces. Their bitterness was overwhelming and what may have been a justified continuance of the war ended up being one of our nation's most noted outlaw gangs. What became known as the James-Younger gang began their activities by riding into Liberty, Missouri, on February 13, 1866, and robbing the Clay County Saving Bank of some $58,000. There were 10 men with the party and a small boy was killed by the crossfire that resulted in the street. Over the next 16 years Jesse and Frank James, Cole, Jim, and Bob Younger, and numerous other associates from their guerrilla days participated in major robberies of banks, trains, and institutions owned by or controlled by Northern interests. Former Confederates and those throughout the nation who had supported the Southern cause embraced the many gallant stories dime novelists created about the James-Younger gang to meet the demands of the emotionally distraught former Confederates. Such fictional portrayals helped create the legends and notoriety the James and Youngers obtained, though such notoriety was not necessarily justified.

Jesse James' war would continue until he was brought down by a shot to the back of the head by Bob Ford on April 3, 1882, for the reward being offered. Jesse was age 34 at the time of his death. Frank James surrendered to Missouri governor Thomas Crittenden in October of 1882. After being tried for past crimes on two occasions and acquitted, Frank returned to society and spent the rest of his life as a model citizen. He died on the James farm near Kearney, Missouri, at age 72 on February 15, 1915.

Bob, Jim, and Cole Younger with their sister Henrietta at the Minnesota State Prison. Embittered over the Confederate defeat, the Youngers, James brothers, and other former members of Quantrill's guerilla forces formed outlaw bands that gained national notoriety. Robbing only from Union-owned banks or railroads, such outlaw gangs became folk heros to many ex-Confederate families throughout the Ozarks. (Photo author's collection)

Cole, Jim, and Bob Younger were all shot to pieces when the gang attempted to rob the bank in Northfield, Minnesota, on September 7, 1876. All three were captured and given terms in the Minnesota State Prison in Stillwater, Minnesota. Bob Younger died of tuberculosis while in prison on September 16, 1889. Jim Younger committed suicide on October 19, 1902, less than one year after his release from prison. Cole completed his sentence and became quite popular traveling around the nation giving speeches on "What Life Has Taught Me," and appearing in various Wild West shows. Cole died of heart failure on March 21, 1916.

Bibliography

Battle of Cabin Creek. Muskogee, OK: Twin Territories Press, 1992.

Brant, Marley. *The Families of Charles Lee and Henry Washington Younger*. Marietta, GA: 1986.

Brant, Marley. *The Outlaw Youngers*. Madison Books, Lanham, MD, and London, England, 1992.

Britton, Wiley. *Memoirs of the Rebellion on the Border, 1863*. Chicago: Cushing, Thomas and Company, 1882.

Britton, Wiley. *Pioneer Life in Southwest Missouri*. Columbia, MO: The State Historical Society of Missouri, 1923.

Britton, Wiley. *The Civil War On the Border 1861-1862*. New York: G. P. Putnam's Sons, The Knickerbocker Press, 1899.

Brownlee, Richard S. *Gray Ghosts of the Confederacy*. Baton Rouge: Louisiana State University Press, 1958.

Castel, Albert. *A Frontier State at War: Kansas, 1861-1865*. Ithaca, NY: Cornell University Press, 1958.

Castel, Albert. *General Sterling Price and the Civil War in the West*. Baton Rouge: Louisiana State University Press, 1968.

Castel, Albert. *The Guerrilla War 1861-1865*. Gettysburg, PA: Historical Times, Inc., 1974.

Cornish, Dudley Taylor. *The Sable Arm*. Lawrence, KS: University Press of Kansas, 1987.

Cottrell, Steve. *Carthage in the Civil War*. Carthage, MO: 1990.

Edwards, John N. *Shelby and His Men*. Cincinnati: Miami Publishing Co., 1867.

Fischer, Leroy H. *The Battle of Honey Springs*. Norman, OK: University of Oklahoma Printing Services, 1988.

Fischer, Leroy H. and Gill, Jerry. *Confederate Indian Forces Outside of Indian Territory*. Norman, OK: University of Oklahoma Press, 1969.

Foote, Shelby. *The Civil War: A Narrative*. Volume 3. New York: Random House, 1974.

Foreman, Grant. *Fort Gibson, A Brief History*. Muskogee, OK: Hoffman-Speed Printing Co., n.d.

Gill, Samuel T. "Rampaging Cavalry Raiders." Military History Magazine's Great Battles. Volume I, Number 2. Leesburg, VA: Empire Press, 1987.

Hughey, Jeffery A. "The Last Stand of the Confederates in Missouri: The Battle of Newtonia." The Midwest Quarterly. Volume XXVII, Number 1, Autumn 1985. Pittsburg, KS: Pittsburg State University, 1985.

Ingenthron, Elmo. *Borderland Rebellion*. Branson, MO: The Ozarks Mountaineer, 1980.

Jones, Samuel. *The Battle of Prairie Grove: December 7, 1862*. Prairie Grove Battlefield Park, Prairie Grove, AR, n.d.

Josephy, Alvin M. *War on the Frontier*. Alexandria, VA: Time-Life Books, Inc., 1986.

Kennell, Everett. "The Battle of Springfield." Springfield, MO: The News-Leader, August 4, 1991.

Marsh, William R. "The Military Career of James G. Blunt: An Appraisal." Unpublished thesis, Kansas State College of Pittsburg, Pittsburg, KS: 1953.

Monaghan, Jay. *Civil War on the Western Border: 1854-1865*. New York: Little, Brown and Company, 1955.

Moneyhon, Carl and Bobby Roberts. *Portraits of Conflict*. Fayetteville, AR: University of Arkansas Press, n.d..

Nevin, David. *The Road to Shiloh*. Chicago: Time-Life Books, Inc., 1983.

Sauer, Carl O. *Geography of the Ozark Highland of Missouri*. Chicago: University of Chicago Press, 1920.

Schrantz, Ward L. *Jasper County, Missouri in the Civil War*. Carthage, MO: The Carthage Press, 1923.

Settle, William A., Jr. *Jesse James Was His Name*. Columbia, MO: University of Missouri Press, 1966, 1977.

Steele, Phillip. *Starr Tracks, Belle and Pearl Starr*. Gretna, LA: Pelican Publishing, 1991.

Steele, Phillip. *Jesse and Frank James, The Family History*. Gretna, LA: Pelican Publishing, 1989.

Turkoly-Joczik, Robert L. "Frémont and the Western Department." Missouri Historical Review. Volume LXXXII, Number 4, July 1988. Columbia, MO: State Historical Society of Missouri, 1988.

United States Congress. *The War of the Rebellion: A Compilation of the Official Records of the Union and Confederate Armies*. Series I, Volume III. Washington, DC: Government Printing Office, 1881.

VanGilder, Marvin L. "Crisis at Carthage." Carthage, MO: The Carthage Press, 1990.

Walker, Wayne T. "Massacre at Baxter Springs." Old West. Volume 19, Number 3, Spring 1983. Iola, WI: Western Publications, 1983.

Wheeler, Keith. *The Scouts*. Alexandria, VA: Time-Life Books, Inc., 1978.

Weaver, Barry Roland. *Jesse James in Arkansas: The War Days*. Arkansas Historical Association Quarterly. Winter 1964, Volume XXIII, Number 4.

Woodward, Grace Steele. *The Cherokees*. Norman, OK: University of Oklahoma Press, 1963.

Younger, Cole. *The Story of Cole Younger By Himself*. 1903. Triton Press, reprint, 1988.

Index

About the Authors

Phillip W. Steele and Steve Cottrell are both natives of the Ozarks. Steele's great-grandfather, Strauther L. Gilliland, enlisted in the Confederate Army in March of 1862 and served in Colonel Whitfield's Texas cavalry. Steele's great-uncle, James A. Roberts, enlisted in the Confederate Army at Fayetteville, Arkansas. He served with the Arkansas cavalry and was assigned to Company C of Crawford's battalion. Cottrell's great-great-great-grandfather, Daniel Jennings, served in the Union forces as a saddler in Company H of the 6th Kansas Cavalry. Proud of their Ozark region family history and having common interests in preserving Ozarks' history, this Reb and Yank hereby present a historical review of the Civil War in the Ozarks.

Steele, a graduate of the University of Arkansas, is the author of seven books on Ozark history, folklore, and Old West subjects. His column, "Hearth Tales of the Ozarks," was featured in the *Ozarks Mountaineer Magazine* for 10 years and greatly contributed to the preservation of the Ozark region's folk heritage. Steele has served as president of the Arkansas Folklore Society, president of Friends of the James Farm, chairman of the Arkansas History Commission, and as a board member of the National Outlaw and Lawman History Association for many years. He also is a member of Western Writers of America and the Ozark Writers' League. More than 100 of his articles on Ozark and Old West historical subjects have been published in major newspapers and magazines throughout the nation. His Heritage Productions company produces documentary films on Ozark and Old West history.

Steve Cottrell, a native of southwest Missouri, is a graduate of Missouri Southern State College. He developed an interest in Civil War history at an early age and his extensive research throughout the Ozarks has resulted in numerous articles on Civil War subjects being published. Cottrell has been active in preservation efforts for Ozark battlefields and has greatly contributed to the region's Civil War museums. As a member of a Missouri re-enactor group he has helped recreate Ozark Civil War skirmishes at various historical events throughout the Ozarks. He has participated in Civil War battle scenes for several films, including the Academy Award-winning film *Glory*.

Authors Phillip W. Steele, left, a native of northwest Arkansas, and Steve Cottrell, a native of southwest Missouri, in front of Elkhorn Tavern at Pea Ridge National Military Park near Garfield, Arkansas. (Photo by authors)